PUFFIN BOOKS

LEGEND OF SPEED

Tim Hanna is the author of two best-selling biographies – *One Good Run*, about Burt Munro, and *John Britten*, the biography of the late New Zealand motorcycle engineering legend. Hanna himself still rides the same Norton Commando Fastback he's owned for the last twenty years and wouldn't consider any other bike – although if he ever makes any money he might allow one of those new Nortons garage space as a backup. He is completing the restoration of a 100-year-old, 45-foot motorsailer sometime soon.

LEGEND OF
SPEED
THE BURT MUNRO STORY

TIM HANNA WITH *DAVID LARSEN*

PUFFIN BOOKS

PUFFIN BOOKS
Published by the Penguin Group
Penguin Group (NZ), 67 Apollo Drive, Rosedale,
North Shore 0632, New Zealand (a division of Pearson New Zealand Ltd)
Penguin Group (USA) Inc., 375 Hudson Street,
New York, New York 10014, USA
Penguin Group (Canada), 90 Eglinton Avenue East, Suite 700, Toronto,
Ontario, M4P 2Y3, Canada (a division of Pearson Penguin Canada Inc.)
Penguin Books Ltd, 80 Strand, London, WC2R 0RL, England
Penguin Ireland, 25 St Stephen's Green,
Dublin 2, Ireland (a division of Penguin Books Ltd)
Penguin Group (Australia), 250 Camberwell Road, Camberwell,
Victoria 3124, Australia (a division of Pearson Australia Group Pty Ltd)
Penguin Books India Pvt Ltd, 11, Community Centre,
Panchsheel Park, New Delhi – 110 017, India
Penguin Books (South Africa) (Pty) Ltd, 24 Sturdee Avenue,
Rosebank, Johannesburg 2196, South Africa
Penguin Books Ltd, Registered Offices: 80 Strand, London, WC2R 0RL, England

First published by Penguin Books (NZ), 2007
Published in Puffin Books, 2007
10 9 8 7 6 5 4 3

Copyright © Tim Hanna, 2007

The right of Tim Hanna to be identified as the author of this work in terms of
section 96 of the Copyright Act 1994 is hereby asserted.
All rights reserved

Photo Acknowledgements
Marty Dickerson: pp 8, 10, 143, 155, 161, 163, 167;
Munro Family Archive: pp 17, 60, 61, 65, 78, 79, 81, 84, 87, 95, 111, 128,
133, 175; Ugo Fadini: pp 118, 120, 121.

Designed by Vivianne Douglas
Typeset by Egan Reid
Printed in Australia by McPherson's Printing Group

All rights reserved. Without limiting the rights under copyright reserved
above, no part of this publication may be reproduced, stored in or
introduced into a retrieval system, or transmitted, in any form or by any
means (electronic, mechanical, photocopying, recording or otherwise),
without the prior written permission of both the copyright owner and
the above publisher of this book.

ISBN: 978 014 330310 7

A catalogue record for this book is available
from the National Library of New Zealand.

www.penguin.co.nz

CONTENTS

ONE	FULL THROTTLE	7
TWO	THE GOD OF SPEED	16
THREE	TOO BIG FOR A BIRD	23
FOUR	POP, POP, POP	29
FIVE	BURT'S FIRST RIDE	33
SIX	RABBIT SHOOTING	38
SEVEN	INTO THE DARK	43
EIGHT	THE INDIAN SCOUT	53
NINE	THE FLYING GOLDTOOTH	59
TEN	AUSTRALIAN SPEEDWAY	64
ELEVEN	GOOD FOR PARTS	70
TWELVE	WHEELS AGAIN	76
THIRTEEN	MOTORCYCLE SALESMAN	82
FOURTEEN	BLOWING UP TREE STUMPS	92

FIFTEEN	FLAT OUT	99
SIXTEEN	FASTEST MAN AROUND	104
SEVENTEEN	FASTER STILL	108
EIGHTEEN	FIRST TRIP TO THE SALT	115
NINETEEN	THE STREAMLINER	124
TWENTY	ONE GOOD RUN	131
TWENTY-ONE	A DATE AT BONNEVILLE	137
TWENTY-TWO	A CHANGE OF PLANS	149
TWENTY-THREE	UTAH AT LAST	154
TWENTY-FOUR	SPEED WEEK	159
TWENTY-FIVE	THE PERFECT RUN	172

CHAPTER ONE

FULL THROTTLE

The old man had to be out of his mind. His motorbike was a battered heap, older than most of the officials standing staring at it. It looked like it might fall to pieces any moment. So did the old man, for that matter – an elderly codger wearing baggy suit pants with the cuffs tucked into his grubby socks, not-quite-worn-out tennis shoes and a weathered, black leather biker jacket, standing next to an ancient machine with smooth red sides and three little fins at the back. What in the world were these two doing on the salt?

The salt: hard-packed underfoot, blinding white in the sunlight, stretching out to the horizon. Flat and hard as your kitchen floor. No trees, no shrubs, not the smallest growing thing. No people. No buildings. Fifteen thousand

The Munro Special.

years ago this landscape had been the floor of a wide salt lake, but the water was long gone. All that was left was the flattest, whitest desert in the world. The great Utah salt flats. Every speed racer's dream. If you wanted to find out how fast you and your machine could go, this was the place, because there was nothing to get in your way. Every year, racers gathered here for Speed Week, the official speed trials where they could set new world records . . . if they were good enough. Not many of them were.

So, what did this old buzzard think he was doing here?

Even his car, a black, humpbacked wreck towing a peculiar home-made trailer, looked like it should have been dragged off the highway in the name of public safety. The dinky little brakes on his bike didn't look capable of slowing down a kid's scooter, so if by some miracle he coaxed the machine up to a respectable speed, he'd have no way of stopping. And he'd need one if things went wrong, which they most likely would. The old man was an obvious danger to himself and to anyone unlucky enough to be standing within a couple of miles of him. What could he possibly hope to achieve, other than embarrassing and possibly killing himself, and wasting a lot of time for a lot of people with better things to do?

He was a joke, and that should have been the end of it. But it wasn't. Somehow he'd wangled permission to do a qualifying run in front of a carload of officials. If they decided he and his outlandish machine were for real, he'd be allowed to compete in the speed trials. The officials were trying not to yawn too obviously. They would putter along behind the old coot until they'd seen enough, and then they'd order him off the salt. With luck, he wouldn't crash.

There was something spooky about the way he stood beside his red, goldfish-shaped bike, one hand resting on its flank as if it were alive and in need of reassurance.

And then he was climbing into it. Its smooth red sides enclosed most of him, as though the goldfish had swallowed him whole, but his back stuck out the top like the goldfish's fin. A team of his friends – obvious misfits, thought the officials – were preparing to give him a push-start. What did they think they were doing, encouraging him like this? People got hurt on the salt.

This was bound to end badly.

The helpers pushed like maniacs. The machine didn't seem to want to budge. Then suddenly the thing roared to life and leapt away, leaving one of the pushers sprawled flat on his face in the salt. The car full of officials had to

Team Indian pushing Burt off.

accelerate hard to catch up. The officials glanced at each other. Surprising! The bike was obviously a bit faster than they'd thought. A bit faster? It was doing about ninety miles an hour! That was slow compared to most of the machines they saw here, but it was about twice as fast as they'd expected from this one. And it was running smoothly, slipping across the shimmering salt like a fish swimming down a river.

Then it gave a lurch. Its rider was groping about in its innards for something. Was he changing gear?

There was a resounding crack. The car's occupants ducked. The machine's rear tire had spat a shower of salt back at them, smacking into the windscreen like shotgun pellets. When they looked up again, they gaped. The old man and his bike were a hundred feet ahead of them! Two hundred! Three! They were going like a stone out of a slingshot!

The official driving the car put his foot hard down, but there was no catching them. They didn't see the old man again until they found him at the other end of the run, standing beside his goldfish-bike, which had its little landing wheels extended.

Earl Flanders, the American Motorcycle Association steward for Speed Week, got out of the car and strolled over. The old guy was looking a bit flustered but, considering he must have been going over 140 miles an hour, that was hardly surprising. Earl nodded at him with a puzzled smile. 'The old girl seemed to run pretty good,' he said.

'You think so, Earl?' replied the old guy. He seemed as surprised as everybody else.

Earl Flanders nodded again. 'She really took off when you changed into top!'

Once more the old guy looked puzzled. 'Top?' he repeated. 'I never got her out of second gear.'

Earl Flanders took a moment to absorb the idea that this old coot had just topped 140 miles per hour *and he hadn't used his bike's fastest gear*. When he eventually located his vocal chords he told the old guy that he was in. He could race the clock with the rest of the competitors. He shook his hand, welcoming him for the first time to the 1962 Speed Week. The old fellow returned the handshake with a numb expression. Most of the officials thought it was probably a reaction to the speed – he probably had never gone so fast before in his life. It must really have taken it out of him.

They were wrong.

Burt Munro loved to travel. He loved to see new places and meet new people. He loved to gas on to them about all his adventures. What he loved most of all, though, was to run his Indian motorcycle. He'd bought it new in 1920 and tuned and rebuilt it ever since to go faster and faster. He was sure that if he could just manage one good run, he could go at least 200 miles an hour.

For the past forty years he had worked on the bike with an almost insanely single-minded determination. Many people thought he was as mad as a meat axe. He had spent uncounted hours in his dimly-lit workshop, melting old bike parts down and pouring them into home-made moulds to make new ones. He often lay awake at night in his narrow little bed in the workshop's dampest corner, with his hand resting on the Indian's tank, thinking about the way gas might flow in a different-shaped combustion chamber. He made overhead valve heads for his machines out of other people's discarded rubbish. Burt Munro could make almost anything.

Sometimes he tapped away for days with a hammer. The bike's aluminium shell alone had taken him five years to patiently knock into shape.

And now the damn thing was threatening to kill him.

He had designed the shell so that when the bike hit high speeds, the wind would flow smoothly over it. Instead, as he approached 150 miles an hour he had felt the Indian start to weave violently from side to side. It had nearly scared the life out of him. He knew what a high-speed accident was like. It was a sickening thing to have the ground and the sky suddenly go spinning and tumbling, and to have the wind thumped out of your body a split-second before the sudden, horrible pain and that final white flash that turned the lights off. Burt had survived enough accidents to last several lifetimes and he hated the sight of blood ... especially his own. A crash at 150 miles an hour could easily have killed him and he'd only avoided it by pure luck.

He'd been sure the carload of officials would decide there and then to ban him from the salt for ever. But it seemed they'd been too far behind and hadn't seen a thing. As he shook Earl Flanders' hand, Burt realised that his rather humble objective would take all the skill he possessed to achieve. All he really wanted was one good run to test his life's work. He just wanted to find out how fast his machine could go.

Although his ability on a motorcycle was in fact a lot greater than anyone in the small crowd might have imagined, the way the Indian was behaving made the outcome disturbingly uncertain. Maybe the wobble would go away as he went faster. Maybe it wouldn't. He hoped it wouldn't get worse, but ... maybe it would.

Ah well, he thought. He was still going to do it. He

was going to get back on the bike when his turn came, get the old thing up into top gear and crack the throttle wide open until it ended . . . one way or another. It might be death, or it might be glory. If it ended up being neither he could always come back the next year.

He shuddered. Burt Munro was a brave man but he was not stupid. There was just no knowing what might happen.

CHAPTER TWO

THE GOD OF SPEED

For as long as he could remember Herbert Munro had hated farming. He especially loathed getting up in the dark on a cold, blustery day to bring in the cows for milking, a chore he had to do every single morning – no exceptions, no excuses – once he turned eight. The farm was a pleasant enough place, as farms went, and his family was generally an okay bunch. His older brother Ernie took the lead and looked out for Herbert, or Burt as his family called him. Of course, Ernie could not guard his young brother against everything. When Burt dived straight off his bed onto his head at the age of three there was nothing Ernie could do except run to fetch their mother. Several anxious hours passed before young Burt finally groaned and opened his eyes, and afterwards, when he was asked why he had thought diving off the bed was a good idea, all the little boy could say was that he didn't know. His mother would later wonder if he had been practising for a lifetime of crashing onto his head.

The family farmed at Edendale, in the far south of New Zealand. The children all worked hard on the farm, both before and after school, but there was still time to climb trees and explore. The boys had three sisters: Eva, the eldest; Ruby, Burt's twin; and little Florence. While the

Burt's family in 1915. Burt is top left.

boys learned to plough behind horses, milk cows, make wooden gates, tighten wire fences, deliver calves and lambs, shear sheep, sort fleeces, stack hay, shoot rabbits, fix leaking irrigation pipes, maintain machinery, and all the other skills a farmer had to master, the girls learned how to be farmer's wives: to sew and cook and clean house. The farm thrived, and all was well with the world at Edendale until the terrible afternoon when the boys and their father went out to chop down a tree.

As the gnarly old pine fell it became caught up in the branches of another tree and stuck there. They went back to the house for lunch and when they came back to finish the job, Ernie, always keen to get on with things, climbed onto the leaning tree and jumped up and down to dislodge it. Before his father could tell him to get off it, the tree ripped loose from its neighbour and crashed to the ground, spinning as it fell. Ernie was caught beneath it and crushed to death.

Burt missed his brother badly, and what made it even worse was the realisation that the farm was now his prison. He was the eldest son. Over the next few years his parents had two more children, Rita and Charlie, and Burt's short time as the family's only son was over. But with Ernie gone, he would always be the *eldest* son. For the eldest son of a farming family there were no choices in life. He was duty-bound to stay home and help his father, and eventually to take over the farm and run it as his own. Burt had always dreamed of grand adventures in distant places and imagined that one day the dreams would become real. That was done with now.

If you had asked Burt why he hated the farm so much, he would have found it hard to answer. He had nothing against the place exactly. He just wasn't happy there. Perhaps it was that the pace of life was so slow. It was the early 1900s and many farmers in the district were bringing in tractors to plough their fields, but Burt's father scorned the things, instead relying on a team of massive Clydesdale horses. On rare occasions Burt managed to get a ride on them and he always tried to choose Tommy. Dolly, Nellie, Bessie, Frankie and Gertie were all good horses but Tommy had spirit. He liked to move! If his father was not looking, Burt would kick the huge beast into action and get him up to full steam. Tommy was surprisingly quick and agile for an animal his size, and he would pound over the farm, clearing gates with his ears pinned back as if it was the best fun in the world. For Burt that was precisely what it was, and the rushing wind filled him with the most exhilarating sense of freedom he had ever known.

His father strongly disapproved of such goings on, however, and he always found out. There was no hiding a gallop on Tommy, because when he really got going the horse's giant hooves dug great holes in the earth at every stride. Later, having survived a severe telling off, Burt would lie in bed and imagine he was flying across the countryside again, free to go where he pleased, never stopping, moving faster and faster. And then, just after he'd fallen asleep it always seemed, it was time to get up and fumble into his rough working clothes before stumbling out into the early dawn darkness to gather the cows for milking again.

Burt was not riding Tommy the day he took the tumble that knocked him out for the second time in his life. He and his father were shifting cattle and Burt was astride one of the mares, carelessly leaning down to latch a gate. The mare suddenly reared up. Burt was caught off guard. His father saw him arc through the air, landing with a tremendous thump to his head on the sun-baked earth. Once more the family waited for Burt to come back to them. This time it was a full twelve hours before he woke up, though afterwards he seemed no worse for wear.

On rare occasions Burt was taken to Invercargill by his father. Travelling by steam train for fifty glorious kilometres was the greatest excitement in his young life. He loved watching the train pull into the platform, steam curling around its wheels like the breath from huddled horses on a cold morning. He would take his seat by the window and wait for the wheels to spin on the rails as the engine heaved into action.

He would watch fences flit past the window so quickly they registered only as a rising and falling blur, while the train rocked back and forth as if impatient to go faster. Arriving was a bad moment, because it meant getting off the train, but there was always the return journey to look forward to.

One rail trip took him and his father a little further, twenty kilometres past Invercargill to the shipping port at Bluff. They were picking up a present for Burt's mother, sent by an aunt in far-away London.

Burt loved every moment of the visit. Tall ships with masts that seemed to scrape the clouds lay next to the docks. Steam cranes and donkey engines hissed and puffed, unloading the ships' holds while sailors watched from the rails.

There were steamships too, dark and squat, with massive iron hull plates lumpy with rivets and streaked with bright rust like freshly dried blood. They smelled of hot oil and coal, like the train. The grassy scent of the ropes made from coconut husks and the ripe smell of fish from a line of trawlers mixed with a sharp aroma from a big, black whaler and wafted on the ocean breeze. A steam tug set out, leaving whirlpools of boiling water astern as she surged into the harbour, her tall funnel billowing black smoke.

It was a doorway into another world. Burt was completely transfixed.

On the train journey home, while his father was in another part of the carriage, Burt slid the wood-framed window up and put his head out into the rushing wind. When his father returned and ordered him to pull it in, with a grim warning about what would happen if the train should suddenly go into a tunnel – 'You'd lose that thick head of yours, boy' – he instantly obeyed. But nothing could wipe the smile from his face. He had sensed something in the raging air tearing past his head. For the first time he had glimpsed the blurred face of the God of Speed.

CHAPTER THREE

TOO BIG FOR A BIRD

When Burt was fourteen he left school and the farm closed around him like a suffocating fog. He was the eldest son. His place was alongside his father, working, working, working. The days merged into an endless round of early mornings and early nights, and his feelings of futility and boredom grew keener. But as far as Burt could see, this was his life. There was nothing for it but to pocket the single shilling his father paid him every week and carry on.

Meanwhile the world was changing. The farm was doing well and Burt's father was able to buy one of the very newest inventions: an electricity generator.

Thousands of generations of humans had lived and died in a world where bright, steady light belonged only to the sun, and now Burt had the power to turn night into day with the flick of a switch.

The farm acquired an electric washing machine, the first in the whole district. People would come on visits just to see it. Burt's father, who still hated the idea of tractors, grudgingly agreed to buy a car. It was a black Model T Ford, and it lived in a special shed built just for it. It was only allowed out on Sundays, for trips to church – and then only if it was fine.

One day Burt was out fixing a fence on a corner of the property when he heard a distant buzzing noise. It was coming from . . . that couldn't be right. It was coming from the sky. Swarming bees? It sounded too far off for that. It was late in the afternoon and the sun was low in the west, shining in his eyes, but . . . he squinted. There was something . . . a small dot. Too big for a bird. It was heading his way. He dropped the wire strainer he'd been using and shielded his eyes so he could see better. The dot drew nearer. Definitely not a bird. But . . . it had two wings! Two *metal* wings!

It was a flying machine.

The engine grew louder and then the thing was sweeping overhead with a roar, waggling its wings awkwardly in response to his wild waving. He could see the pilot sitting inside it! He watched it disappear over the low hills, the beat of its engine fading into the afternoon's silence, then picked up the wire strainer and turned back to his work.

The whole world was breaking into a gallop while he was forced to stand still.

Burt grew taller. He finally ended up not quite making it to six feet, which annoyed him. But he remembered the flying machine. There were more ways than one to gain a bit of altitude. Burt decided to build a glider.

He had noticed a stand of large bamboo growing on the roadside near the front gate to the McLean's place, a mile or so down the road. One Sunday afternoon he set off with a saw and began collecting bamboo poles. That evening he spent several hours in the big shed, happily cutting up old kerosene tins. He knew exactly how his aircraft should look. With the bamboo, the metal from the tins, and a lot of fencing wire, he had everything he needed.

His father thought the idea was a pure waste of time, but he was no fool. It was obvious Burt was unhappy on the farm. The boy needed to learn some sense. It might do him good to try his hand at this mad project and fail . . .

Give him a chance to figure out he belonged on the ground, settle him down a bit. When Burt returned to his task the next evening he was left alone to get on with it.

After a month, the craft had a skeletal frame, much like the one Burt had observed on the plane. There was a single main wing, sixteen feet from tip to tip. Three bamboo poles formed the main part of the glider's body, with shorter bits of bamboo holding them together. The tail was shaped like the feathers on a dart. The wing was made up of two thick bamboo spars, with bamboo ribs every two feet. These were held in place by a single long, thin piece of beech wood. Burt had spent nearly a week's worth of evenings cutting this out of a fallen beech tree, using the same saw he had used to cut the bamboo.

Although Burt was more or less making up the glider as he went along, it began to take shape. Burt went to his father to ask if he could take some old canvas he had found and use it as his machine's outer hide. The request brought his father up short. The boy had got a lot further than he had expected, if he was up to covering the glider's framework already.

Burt's father was not a cruel man, but he had very firm ideas about how life should be. His son needed to learn that his place was on the farm. If he actually succeeded in making this crazy contraption fly, it would teach him precisely the wrong lesson. And if he flew it and it crashed . . . The family had already had to deal with Ernie's death.

He went out to the shed with his son and looked the glider over. He had to admit it: Burt was making a good job of it. He thought for a moment. Then he gave Burt a flat, no-nonsense order. This monster was to be dismantled immediately.

It was the most devastating moment of Burt's life.

He pleaded with his father. Could he just finish the glider, even if only to see whether it would fly with no pilot?

Absolutely not.

Well, could he fly it down a sloping cable, strung from the top of one tree to the base of another? It would be better than nothing.

His father pointed out that that would prove nothing beyond the willingness of an object to slide down a slope and smash itself against a solid object. Hardly worth the price of a bolt of good canvas.

Burt knew then that his cause was lost. The world might be changing in a lot of ways, but a father still had the right to expect absolute obedience from his family. It was just the way things were.

He set about taking his creation apart with the same

care he had used putting it together. The fencing wire was rolled back up and stored for mending fences. The bamboo poles were lugged back up the road and returned to Mr McLean, who had not noticed they were gone and was somewhat surprised by their return. The carefully cut and shaped pieces of kerosene tin were placed in a box of odds and ends and saved in case they were ever needed for something. Nothing was wasted.

There was no time for self-pity on the Munro farm. Burt swallowed his biting disappointment and got on with things.

CHAPTER FOUR

POP, POP, POP

Burt's mother was determined her children should grow up knowing how to sing and dance. At least once a week she would sit down at the family piano and play, and her three older daughters were expected to sing along with the music. Burt, to his own surprise, found he loved these evenings, though it was a relief that he was rarely asked to sing himself. Neither he nor his father had much of a singing voice.

But his father could dance. He could dance like a dream. Burt discovered this the day another amazing new machine arrived on the farm: an automatic player piano.

There were no CDs in Burt's world, no tape recorders, no radios. If you wanted music, you learned to play an instrument. But the mechanical piano changed that. Suddenly it was possible to have music playing even if Burt's mother stood up from the keyboard and danced with her husband. The sight of his parents gliding effortlessly around the room together, while the piano played away by itself, was pure enchantment. Burt and his sisters never spoke about it, but he knew they felt the same. Soon all the family were learning dance steps – the waltz, the foxtrot, the quickstep, the polka. Burt discovered that he liked it. In those years, trapped on the farm, the family dance sessions were one of the few things he had to look forward to.

A short while after the arrival of the magical piano, Burt was in town doing something for his father when he saw a very unusual bike. Everyone rode bikes in that part of New Zealand, partly because cars were still very expensive, but this bike was larger and moved like an eel, threading quickly through the other bikes and the horse traffic cluttering the wide main street of Invercargill. A thin stream of oily smoke trailed behind it. It made a little puttering noise as it went along: pop, pop, pop . . . why, the thing had a motor attached to it!

In spite of it being a hot summer day, the rider was wearing heavy boots, an oilskin coat, gloves, a tight-fitting leather hat and goggles. Burt had a moment of pure jealous rage. The man was dressed for the open road. With get-up like that, he could ride to the ends of the earth! Why should Burt be shackled to the farm when there were machines like this and a whole world out there to explore?

After that, the gentle pop, pop, pop of the motorbike kept intruding on his thoughts.

Later that year, the First World War broke out in Europe. It was half a world away, but many of the settler families of New Zealand still thought of Europe as their real home. Burt's parents received visits from neighbours whose sons had proudly signed up to fight for England and sailed off to join the British army. Some were scarcely older than Burt, who was fifteen that year. You had to be eighteen to join up, but he knew there were boys his own age who were volunteering and lying about their age. No one tried to stop them.

His father made it clear, however, that as far as he was concerned his son's duty lay at home. Now, more than ever, he announced, the British Empire will need food. A farmer's job was to stay on the farm and grow crops. The soldiers would need feeding. The same neighbours who had so willingly sent their own sons to the fighting under-stood the need to keep farm production up, and there was no resentment at the idea of Burt staying behind.

So when the Munro family went to town to watch more than 300 young men marching off to the special train waiting for them at the city's grand wooden station, Burt waved and cheered with everybody else and then went home. The endless cycle of work was still there waiting for him. The war would be over by Christmas, everyone agreed. Just one more adventure Burt would never experience.

CHAPTER FIVE

BURT'S FIRST RIDE

The war had been going for a year when Burt's neighbour
Eon McLean came over to visit, riding a brand new motorcycle. Burt couldn't take his eyes off it. He asked question
after question about how it worked and what the parts
were called, most of which his neighbour had no idea
how to answer. His father rescued the man by inviting
him in for a cup of tea, telling Burt, 'Go find something
useful to do.'

Find something useful to do? Maybe later . . . Burt
began inspecting every detail of the motorcycle, imagining
himself riding it, bouncing along gently on the rich-
chestnut leather saddle. It was beautifully built. Burt was

particularly interested in the system of springs designed to reduce bumps as you rode, and it took him only a few minutes to figure out how they worked. He also admired the large exposed flywheel and the leather belt driving a big pulley on the rear wheel.

He was still on his knees in the dust peering at the engine, his hands running over the warm metal lovingly, when the two older men emerged. Mr McLean brushed Burt's father's apologies aside and said that Burt was welcome to come over some time and have a ride. And then with a gentle kick of the starter pedal he was off, the bike spitting up a little rooster tail of gravel as it accelerated down the drive.

A chance to take up the invitation came sooner than Burt had dared hope. Visitors were coming to stay, a rare event in the Munro house. Burt's mother had cousins in Dunedin and it was years since she had seen them. They had never been to the farm, so Burt's father arranged to meet them at the turnoff from the main road and escort them along the narrow metal road to the Munro farm. But when the day came the family's treasured car refused to start.

Burt spotted his opportunity. He offered to ride a horse over to the McLean's place to ask if he could borrow the motorcycle, then take it down to the main road to meet the visitors. There was a long pause while his father thought it over. To Burt's amazement, he agreed. Burt had a halter on Tommy and was away over the paddocks at a good gallop before his father had time to change his mind.

When Mr McLean heard about the emergency he immediately wheeled the bike out and showed Burt the brake, the throttle, the choke, the fuel cock and the starting technique. It was an easy machine to get started and Burt soon had the hang of it. After a couple of loops of the circular driveway he was off down the road with the wind in his hair.

He had never been so excited in his life.

The day was warm. He could hear the drone of cicadas and smell the fresh scent of the roadside bracken as he gradually opened the throttle wider and wider. Soon he was flying along, listening to the gentle blat, blat of the bike's engine. There were several spots where the road went through shallow river fords and Mr McLean had warned him not to go too fast through them. If the cold water splashed up into the hot engine, the shock could crack the metal. He eased his way through the first of the fords with hardly a splash, then it was back up to full speed, leaning the machine into the steeply banked corners and laughing out loud for the pure joy of it.

His exhilaration lasted only a couple more kilometres

before the machine suddenly chugged to a halt. He carefully propped it up on its stand and stepped back to glare at it. What was the problem? He waited for the answer to leap to mind. It didn't. A careful examination of the wires and leads revealed no obvious problems and the tank was still brimming with petrol. He climbed back on and tried to start it, kicking the starter again and again. And again. And again. He was going to be late . . . his father would never let him ride the bike again. He kicked the starter. He kicked it again. The machine burst back into life. He was off! Though the engine sounded a little less sure than it had . . .

It stopped again. This was not good. He kicked and kicked and kicked at the starter. His foot got so tired he had to stop. *He was going to be late.* He gave one last gentle prod on the starter. The bike burst back to life again.

Right. So this was a machine that liked to have naps. The next time it stopped he simply waited ten minutes and, sure enough, it started faultlessly. Stopping and starting and stopping and starting, he limped his way to the meeting point. He got there just in time.

He gave his uncle and aunt precise instructions on how to reach the farm, just in case the bike died again before he could lead them there. It did. He waved them on past him, and waited happily for the little machine to get its breath back, which, sure enough, it did. When he eventually made it back to Mr McLean's he found the farmer looking concerned. 'I forgot to tell you about the bloody oil pump,' he exclaimed. 'You have to give it a pump every now and then or it will break down!'

Burt explained how he'd dealt with the problem and Mr McLean was pleased to see that the bike was still running sweetly. As he rode Tommy home, Burt knew that he had to have his own bike. He leaned forward and laid his head on the horse's neck, speaking softly into its ear, 'Two and a half horsepower, Tommy. That little egg of a thing contains two and a half of you!' He sat up and slapped the horse's rump. Tommy shambled into a gallop and then seemed to catch the boy's mood, lengthening his strides until he was pounding across the fields, throwing up clods of wet earth.

His father was going to complain when he saw those deep hoofprints in his fields, especially since they had obviously been made on the way home, after the emergency was over and there was no excuse to hurry. Burt would handle it with his usual mumbled apology and all would soon be forgotten. Unlike the memory of a fine morning spent riding a motorcycle with the wind whistling through his hair. That, Burt could already tell, would remain with him for the rest of his life.

CHAPTER SIX

RABBIT SHOOTING

Fifty years before Burt was born, English settlers had decided it would be a good idea to let rabbits loose in New Zealand. It would be a nice reminder of home and the little things would make good eating. New Zealand has no natural predators for rabbits, and by the time Burt was born, the creatures had become a plague. Many farmers, particularly sheep farmers on the vast high-country stations, were forced to walk off their land for ever, because the rabbits were eating all the grass and the sheep were starving to death. Once the grass was gone, there were no roots to help hold the earth in place. When heavy rains came, the soil simply washed away. Parts of the countryside began to look like as barren and bare as the surface of the moon.

Farmers tried bringing in ferrets, weasels and stoats to eat the rabbits. But New Zealand has many species of flightless birds, which turned out to be much easier for the predators to catch. They mostly left the rabbits alone. Cats were released into the high country, but they were as fond of an all-bird diet as the ferrets, stoats and weasels.

Burt had been shooting rabbits since he was nine years old, usually at twilight when the animals came out of their holes to eat. He was allowed to use the farm's rifle and all the ammunition he needed. It was boring, because the rabbits simply sat about waiting to be shot, but he had a good eye and seldom wasted a bullet. And his lonely rambles at least got him out of the house.

One evening while he was taking aim at a foraging rabbit, he heard a shot from a shallow gully half a kilometre away. His target raised its head in alarm and scampered off. A little annoyed and very curious, Burt trotted towards where the shot had sounded. He found a young man down on one knee skinning a rabbit, his rifle slung across his shoulder. He looked up in surprise when Burt challenged him, but calmly completed his task and stood up. He carefully folded the rabbit pelt and placed it in a bag hanging from his belt. Only then did he look directly at Burt. 'You'd be Burt Munro,' he said.

Burt demanded to know what the stranger was doing on his father's land. The boy was about the same age as Burt but a little stockier. Like Burt, he was dressed in working clothes and he looked friendly enough. He told Burt politely that his name was Jack Murdoch and that his father owned the property on the other side of the McLeans' place. He apologised for being on Munro land without permission but said he didn't think anyone would mind him shooting a few bunnies. Jack shrugged his rifle into a comfortable position and held out his hand.

'I'd like to stay and chat,' he said, 'but I have a bit of a tramp to get home.'

Burt shook his hand. 'You're the first bloke I ever saw out here apart from my father. I won't say anything but he probably wouldn't like you being here.'

Jack paused and seemed to come to a decision. 'There's this chap who buys my pelts and pays me good money,' he said. 'I could show you how to prepare them if you want. We could do a bit of shooting together and you could make a bit of extra money. Interested?'

Jack Murdoch was as good as his word. He showed Burt how to make simple frames to stretch the pelts and how to treat them with rock salt so they didn't start to smell. He took all of Burt's finished skins to his buyer, paying Burt exactly what he was owed. Burt enjoyed the company and they met nearly every day just before dusk. They did very well together.

Burt's father seemed happy with his son's sudden enthusiasm for shooting, but insisted that since Burt was now making money with the farm's gun, he had to pay for his own ammunition. Even so, by the end of the first month Burt had made almost a pound, which was nearly as much as he had saved from his farm wages in the whole previous year. Hunting with Jack quickly became a big part of his life. He still greeted each dark morning with a groan, but getting out of bed to fetch the cows in seemed a little less painful now he had hunting with Jack to look forward to.

The passing seasons brought little good news from the war. More and more young men left the district to fight, and more and more families grieved for the ones who didn't come back. In spite of the terrible reports from the front, Burt and Jack decided they would walk off their fathers' farms and join up when they turned eighteen. Burt was nine months older than Jack and he agreed to wait until they could go together. The truth was that Burt was more nervous of defying his father than he was of being blown up on the Western Front.

Just a few weeks before Jack's eighteenth birthday, the paper reported that Germany had surrendered. The war was over. Burt and Jack had spent most of their teenage years with the war raging somewhere over the horizon, always expecting that one day it would reach out for them. Now, as mysteriously as it had started, it had finished. There were celebrations, but they were quiet ones. The victory was far away and had little to do with day-to-day life, and too many of the district's sons would never be coming home.

Burt and Jack carried on shooting together for a couple of months. Then one night, as the family were sitting down to dinner, Burt's father quietly said something unbelievable. Burt was sure he must have misheard. He asked his father to repeat it, which his father obligingly did. He spoke slowly and firmly so that there could be no confusion.

'I have sold the farm.'

CHAPTER SEVEN

INTO THE DARK

Burt's father did not bother to explain his decision. The farm was sold and that was that. Burt wondered when he was older if perhaps it was something his father had been wanting to do for years, but had put off until the war was over. Certainly the need to keep the farm running had always been his excuse for keeping Burt away from the fighting.

But that day, Burt didn't stop to ask questions. Only one thing mattered.

He was free.

Free to leave, to travel, to see the world and do whatever he liked in it! He had managed to save a little money from his farm wages and a bit more from the rabbit business. It was a good start. He went off immediately to tell Jack the news. His friend promised to go with Burt on his travels, at least as far as Christchurch. Christchurch was the largest city in the South Island – an exciting destination for two lads whose only previous city experiences were day-trips to the tiny town of Invercargill.

When the time came to leave, Burt said his goodbyes in a daze, hardly hearing his mother's warnings about the dangers of the big city. His father said little as he drove his son and Jack to Invercargill. He shook both boys by the hand solemnly and left them at the train station without a backward glance.

They went first to Dunedin, where they were to change trains to the more powerful express. The Dunedin railway station left them both completely speechless. A gleaming white ceiling floated above rich mosaic floors. There were high stained-glass windows depicting onrushing trains, and the white light streaming in looked as though it was being beamed out of the trains' headlights. It was a magical effect and it held Burt spellbound. If he could travel just a few hours and find something this wonderful, what might the rest of the world hold?

Then and there, he made a vow to find out.

Christchurch was a lot of fun, no doubt about it. Within half an hour of arriving Burt and Jack had found a comfortable little boarding house in the middle of the city. They explored everything, visiting places like the museum nearly every day for three weeks. On hot days they caught the trolley bus to New Brighton and swam in the surf and had sandwiches for lunch. Every night they found a dance where Burt could show off the skills his mother had taught him on the polished floor.

The young men's money lasted most of the summer, but finally they had to look for work. They were sitting on the grassy bank of the River Avon, the clear ribbon of water that ran through the city, when Jack announced his intention to catch the train to Banks Peninsula and get a job on a farm.

Burt lay back with a sigh and closed his eyes.

'Jack,' he said, 'if I never see another farm in my life it will be too soon. It's taken me eighteen years to escape one and I'm blowed if I want to just give up and go back to another! I've had a gutsful of cows and that's a fact.'

Jack assured Burt that farming would be just a temporary thing. They would save up their money and then move on. Maybe even to Australia! But Burt was not keen to have cows once more ruling his life.

'If we have to we have to, Jack, but I'd rather pull my own head off and drop rocks down my neck.'

That night as the two boys were having dinner for

the last time at their boarding house, a new man joined them. He became increasingly talkative as they ate, entertaining them with tales of his time working on the Otira Tunnel.

Everybody knew about the tunnel, of course. It was the longest anywhere in the British Empire, and had so far been more than twelve years in the making. The South Island of New Zealand has a mighty range of mountains running down its spine, cutting the island into two halves. The tunnel was intended to link the halves together, letting trains travel between Christchurch and Greymouth on the West Coast.

Workers on the tunnel lived in a village on a flat bit of ground above the Otira River. The place was called the Island and, according to their new friend, it was a grand spot to live and an even better one to work. He asked what Jack and Burt did to earn their living. Jack told him that they were off in the morning to find work on a farm. The man snorted. Farming was all right for those who owned the farm, he supposed, but it was an awful job for the hired hands. Working all hours, paid hardly anything and fed tough old mutton. If you were going to be stuck in the middle of nowhere, he said, you might as well make some money. Two strong blokes like them could be making two and a half pounds a week in the tunnel.

Burt leaned forward eagerly. That was almost as much as he had earned in a year at home! That night he could not sleep.

Jack had made it clear that he was not interested in being a cave troll for a living, and if Burt wanted to go to the tunnel, he was on his own. In the morning they argued about it over breakfast until Burt at last proposed that they toss a coin. 'Heads for the tunnel, tails for the cows,' he said laughing. Jack shook his head. He wasn't going underground on the toss of a coin or anything else. Burt flipped a penny anyway. It was heads.

An hour later they were at the station. Jack was going east, Burt west. The departure of the train for Little River was announced and Jack hefted his bag. Burt's train would be another hour. They shook hands solemnly and Jack shook his head sadly.

'I wish you'd change your mind,' he said. 'We could still do a bit of shooting.'

Burt hooted. 'No more farms for me!' He clapped his friend on the shoulder. 'I'll say hello to any bunnies I come across at the Island and tell them to keep an eye out for you.'

The whistle sounded and Jack swung up the steps as the train began to move. He turned back to wave and then he was gone. It was the last time Burt ever saw him.

Working on the tunnel turned out to be a great adventure and the pay was just as good as Burt had hoped. It was always cold and usually wet, and the terrible darkness inside the mountain range was relieved only by a few feeble electric lights strung from the dripping ceiling. But it wasn't cow farming. For that, Burt was willing to overlook a great deal of discomfort. And he enjoyed living at the Island, even if the huge mountains all around shut out most of the sunlight. The place could feel pretty bleak at times, with the deep blue of the Otira River tumbling down its rocky channel and the grey, shadowed scree slopes eternally slipping towards the valley floor, while the dark, jagged, snow-spattered ridges thrust into the clouds above. But Burt was seldom unhappy. Even when a bitter southerly blew up the valley, freezing everything in its path, he remained cheerful.

Altogether the life suited him. His new workmates teased each other constantly. It would have been stupid to take offence and few ever did. Burt discovered he had a good sense of humour and a was able to laugh at himself. He would probably have been happy to carry on at the Island for years, but fate had other plans. After only a year and a half, his freedom vanished as suddenly as it had arrived.

During his time on the tunnel project, Burt had

received a letter every week from his mother telling him the family news and he had tried to write back at least once a month. It seemed the family had been happily living with his grandparents, his father working on his own father's farm. The arrangement seemed to be working well enough, but it struck Burt as odd. He never quite knew why his father had sold their farm. Perhaps there had been money problems. But his father was a farmer to the bone and he was pretty sure he would buy another farm if he could manage it.

Burt was right. One day he was called to the engineer's site office and handed an urgent telegram. His father had bought a new farm and wanted him to come and work on it. Immediately.

Burt did not think for a single moment that he was free to say no. This was his father. When your father said work, you worked.

He signed a resignation form, arranged for the pay he was owed to be sent on, packed, made his farewells and left. He was leaving a job that paid 125 pounds a year to return home to work for a miserable shilling a week.

But it was wonderful to see his family again and it was surprisingly easy to fit back into the old routines. Elston Lea, as the new farm was called, was on the outskirts of Invercargill. Burt's first task was to help his father build a new farmhouse. The job gave Burt a lot of pleasure. He had always enjoyed working with timber and it was satisfying to show his father the new skills he had learned building scaffolding in the Otira Tunnel. When the house was finished it was something very special: large, graceful, with airy rooms and a lot of space for everyone. Once the family were under their new roof and farming was under way again, Burt had time to think hard about his future.

There were no immediate prospects of escape. But the new farm was much closer to town than the old one had been and he had money in the bank now. He could have some fun in his evenings, at least. Hungry for company and eager to meet girls, he took the trolley bus to town most nights to go dancing. He regularly missed the last trolley bus home and cheerfully walked back through the night, humming a tune under his breath, his coat buttoned up against the cold.

As well as meeting a lot of young women, who were impressed with his skills on the dance floor, Burt also made many new friends among the young men at the dances. Some of these men owned motorbikes. Motorbikes had become wildly popular throughout New Zealand over the past few years, being much cheaper than cars and much faster than horses. There was always a good collection of bikes outside the dance hall and Burt slowly became familiar with the different makes and models.

Ever since his experience with his neighbour's bike, Burt had dreamed of having another ride. His opportunity came at last when one of his new friends offered him a go on his almost brand-new bike, a shiny silver Norton. He and another mate were going to a dance at a small country hall about seventy kilometres out of town. If Burt was keen he could ride the Norton on the way up while the owner sat on the back of his mate's bike. They would swap for the return journey, which would be in the dark and a bit more dangerous.

It was a generous offer and Burt was quick to accept. The ride was astonishing. The other bike took off like a startled hare and Burt had to keep the Norton's throttle wide open most of the time to keep up. They were travelling faster than he would have thought possible, and at every corner he expected the Norton to slide sidewise and crash. But it flew smoothly through the gravel, jiggling up and down like an excited pony out for a trot. Though no pony ever trotted half as fast as this. By the time they got to the dance Burt knew for sure that he had to have a bike of his own.

There were quite a few to choose from. Not knowing too much about what made a good bike, he asked his friends for advice. Unfortunately they all disagreed. In the end, Burt bought his first bike mainly because he liked the colour – bright blood red. It was called a Clyno and it cost him fifty pounds, the most money he had ever spent on anything.

His father was deeply disappointed and made no effort to hide the fact. He regarded the motorcycle as a dangerous waste of time, the kind of thing only a spoilt rich brat would throw away his money on. He complained non-stop for weeks. He refused even to look at the machine.

This suited Burt fine. To be honest, he barely even heard his father's complaints. He was happier than he had ever been. The big, elegant Clyno was quite a powerful machine and he had many memorable dashes around the countryside with his growing band of motorcycling mates. He continued to go to dances every night and now that he had the Clyno he never had to worry about walking home if he stayed out too late. He took to telling his motorcycling friends that there were only two speeds in life: 'Flat out and faster!'

CHAPTER EIGHT

THE INDIAN SCOUT

Burt accepted many invitations to roar about the country with other motorcyclists. Any excuse would do if it got them out on the road. One fine summer day he was part of a small group that set out to visit a sick friend. The rush to get there was so exciting that the riders somehow forgot to stop. They zipped on past their friend's gate and into the hills, finally pausing to admire the view from a peak.

As they headed back down, Burt was riding next to a relative of his named Hugh, who was just a few years older than he was despite being one of his uncles. Hugh's bike, a New Imperial, had developed a misfire and he was struggling to keep up. Burt slowed down to make sure Hugh made it home. From time to time he had to pause to let Hugh catch up and while he was waiting he amused himself by practising stunts. As they were coming out of the foothills, Hugh came around a corner to see his nephew rolling briskly down a gentle slope with the bike in neutral, standing on the seat with his arms outstretched.

Hugh nursed his ailing machine alongside and yelled at his grinning nephew. 'Who the heck do you think you are? Jesus Christ on a motorcycle?'

Burt grinned, flipped him a smart salute and promptly fell off, landing heavily on top of his head. Hugh skidded to a stop. Burt must have broken his neck! He dumped the New Imperial on its side and ran back to where Burt was lying stretched out on the road. Burt was breathing evenly, as if he were fast asleep. There was no blood anywhere. Hugh pulled him over onto the grass at the side of the road and rolled up his coat to make a pillow. The Clyno puttered away happily in the background until it finally coughed and stopped. The afternoon was suddenly very, very quiet.

There was little Hugh could do except to make Burt comfortable and hope another vehicle came along. He retrieved both machines and placed them on their stands, grabbing a picnic blanket out of his saddlebag to cover Burt. Dusk began to fall.

It was nearly dark when Burt groaned and wearily sat up. His eyes slowly focused on the two machines standing in the gathering gloom. He gave a puzzled sigh and then noticed the worried Hugh.

'Oh, hello Hugh,' he said. 'It was good of you to wait.' He rubbed his head and then calmly stood up. 'Well come on. We need to get home.'

With so many motorcycles around, organised bike races were becoming frequent events. Burt went to every one he could. They were mostly held on the two local beaches, partly because it was hard to get permission to race on the roads, but mostly because the beaches offered firm, flat sand that ran for miles between streams and river mouths. For much of the year both beaches were clear of driftwood and seaweed, and car and motorcycle owners could race as hard and as often as they liked.

There were also races on grass at the southern country fairs. The competition was fierce and by the time Burt joined the fray, speeds of more than seventy miles an hour were common. At those speeds the bumpy grass surfaces were lethal. It was unusual for a race to be completed without at least one rider falling off his bike, and when that happened there was a real chance another rider might crash into him. Competitors skidded sideways around the oval turns at each end of the tracks, with their throttles wide open and their rear tyres spitting a wake of stones and torn-up grass. If someone fell during a turn it nearly always brought other bikes down as well, in a tangle of tumbling wheels, arms and legs.

Serious injuries were rare but they did happen. To the crowds it always looked as though they might occur at any moment. On the one occasion Burt's mother saw grass-track racing, during the Invercargill Country Fair, she was so horrified she begged her son to give up riding altogether. Burt grinned and promised he would always be careful, which was not quite what his mother had hoped to hear.

Burt was fond of his Clyno, but it took another bike to give him a bad case of love at first sight. He was passing the Criterion Hotel car park and saw her sitting there. She was red, but not a bold, bright red like the Clyno. A lovely quiet red. The elegant writing on her side announced that she was an Indian.

Burt looked her over. He patted the rich, tan leather seat, testing the spring and smiling as the saddle bounced back against his palm. She had a simple and solid design, and he got down on one knee, like a man asking a woman to marry him, so as to have a proper look at the shape of her cast alloy case. Like everything else about her, it was beautiful.

He stood and walked back a few paces, never taking his eyes off her. She was a beauty all right, and when you fired her up she'd really go, he reckoned. No doubt about it. He realised she already belonged to someone else, but all was not lost. There would be a twin sister somewhere, and by God she would be his.

He knew just who to see. One of his new friends, Archie Prentice, was a motorcycle salesman. Burt reluctantly dragged himself away from the beauty in the car park and made his way to Archie's modest showroom. Archie was always pleased to see him, but today he was even more pleased than usual. So, Burt wanted to buy a bike.

Red was it? Ah yes, that would be the brand spanking new Indian Scout. Just a few in the country but there are a couple more on the way from the United States. A lovely thing. Quite a demand for them. Anyone wanting one would need to pay me a bit in advance.

How much? Oh, not too much – only 150 pounds. Yes, yes, I know, but you get what you pay for, don't you. Of course, the electric headlight adds 10 pounds to the price over the acetylene unit. No, nothing wrong with acetylene lights. Done the trick up till now, haven't they? Okay, 140 pounds then.

And you want the exact same colour. Indian Red!

Burt's father was going to be furious, but . . . he'd get over it. Burt was twenty-one years old now. Old enough and ugly enough to spend his own money on anything he liked.

CHAPTER NINE

THE FLYING GOLDTOOTH

Burt's Indian took only a month to arrive. By the time it had been carefully broken out of its wooden shipping crate in Archie's modest workshop, the old Clyno had gone to its proud new owner, the local blacksmith – for exactly the same money Burt had paid for it. When he took the money from the blacksmith and gave Archie the remainder of what he owed him for the Indian, he was left holding just a few limp notes. He was now almost completely broke. But as he carefully checked over his new machine, he felt like the richest man in town.

The design of the Indian Scout was fairly standard – no bad thing at a time when many manufacturers

Burt and his new Indian in 1923.

built questionable design features into their bikes simply
to look different. But the Scout also used the absolute
best technology of the day. The engine was simple but
effective, and power was transmitted to the back wheel by
a chain – a far better system than the leather belt drives
used on many bikes.

Like the rest of the machine, the sturdy frame
represented the best contemporary thinking. It had been
designed to provide a comfortable and reliable ride over
the bumpy, stony roads that were still common in those
days. It was solidly engineered for a comfortable ride and
it took only a few minutes for Burt to confirm his first
impressions. The machine ran silky smooth, and when
you gunned the throttle she took off like a rocket. By

the end of the week Burt had covered several h
kilometres and was infatuated with his new bike.

Nearly every night Burt fired up the Indian and headed
out dancing. They were high-spirited evenings with
endless practical joking and Burt was always at the heart
of the party. He and his motorcycling mates enjoyed
giving one another nicknames and Burt soon had one of
his own. Like many people in those days, he had a number
of gold fillings, some of which were easy to see whenever
his mouth was open. He became known as the Flying
Goldtooth.

One night Burt agreed to ride as a passenger behind
his mate Burt Martyn, who had a 350cc Indian Prince, to

Burt's beloved machine.

Riverton, twenty-eight kilometres out of town. The dance there turned out to be boring and the two friends headed home earlier than usual. The little Prince was struggling under Burt's extra weight and about halfway home, at Wrights Bush, a small village with a hall and not much else, the bike sputtered and stopped dead. They pushed the machine into the weak pool of light from the single bulb hanging over the hall door and spread out the roll of tools every biker carried. From inside the hall the tinkle of a badly played piano could only just be heard over the clomping of many feet. Clearly the dance here was going better than the one they had just left.

The pair very quickly found the trouble. The bike's clutch had slipped out of place, but Burt reckoned he could fix it well enough to get home, if they could just find something to hold it together with. He thought for a moment. Then he slipped inside the hall and returned a moment later carrying a smart trilby hat. He quickly cut off the brim with his clasp-knife and handed it to his surprised friend.

'Hell's bells, Burt. Someone's going to be pretty annoyed when it's time to go home!'

Burt chortled. 'Well, it could have been worse.'

'How?'

'The hat could have belonged to one of us!'

Martyn shook his head and, shooting nervous glances at the door, began putting the clutch back together, using the hat brim to hold it in place. They were soon ready to go on, but first Burt insisted on returning the remains of the hat to its hook inside the hall. The Prince carried them home with no more trouble, and the hat brim was still giving good service months later. Martyn must have told the story to a mate, because the next time Burt walked into the public bar in town to meet his friends, someone yelled out, 'Hold on to your hats, boys! The Flying Goldtooth has arrived!'

CHAPTER TEN

AUSTRALIAN SPEEDWAY

His life as the Flying Goldtooth was the only high spot left in Burt's existence. Years were slipping by, one after another, with nothing to show for them but more early mornings getting the cows in. It was a waste of a man's life.

His friends were all getting married. Marriage, Burt began to see, was something his parents expected from him, although they never mentioned it. If he were married, that would mean making a new life with his wife. Finding a place to live.

Leaving the farm.

No more cows.

Beryl on the bike with Gwen and Margaret in the sidecar.

His father would have no objection to him leaving if it was to get married . . .

His friend Burt Martyn had a sister called Beryl. She was pretty, she was quiet, she was kind. And Burt had always been welcome at her home and counted her family as friends.

He liked her. He really liked her quite a lot.

Before very long, Burt and Beryl were married and off on the biggest adventure of Burt's life. The idea of leaving the farm had caught fire inside his head. He could go anywhere. He could even leave the country! They could go to Australia, where the wages were as big as the enormous land mass itself. It would mean saying goodbye to all his friends, and to raise the fare he would have to sell the Indian. That made him stop and think, but he had to do it. There would be other Indians. This was his chance to escape and see the world. Best to bite the bullet and fly! The couple were soon aboard a small steamer heading for the city of Melbourne, across the Tasman Sea.

Australia was booming. There was plenty of work for a handyman to get his teeth into and the wages were good. Burt was soon employed as a carpenter and with many new buildings going up in Melbourne he was seldom short of work.

Soon Burt and Beryl had a daughter, June. Burt doted

on his little girl, but he was restless at home. Bikes had returned to the centre of Burt's life, and he was often to be found at the nearest racetrack.

In Melbourne he had become a speedway fan. The city had a famous mile-long, hard-surface speedway track where riders could really open up their machines. It was a dangerous place and often attracted up to 10,000 spectators, many of whom went along hoping to see accidents. More often than not, they got their wish.

Burt introduced himself to the racers and met the local Indian salesman. He offered to help out at the track by fixing any machines that needed quick repairs and, before long, he was being offered machines to race. The best way to sell bikes was to prove they were fast, safe and cheap to run. There were lots of different races designed to help do this, some of them tests of speed, some of them tests of hill-climbing ability and some of them tests of how far the bikes could go on a single gallon of petrol. A skillful, utterly fearless man like Burt was the perfect rider for these races and opportunities began to come his way. He took full advantage of them all.

Once, he won an economy run by coaxing an Indian Scout to go 116 miles on a single gallon. But this sort of careful riding was not the sort he really enjoyed. He preferred speed runs and hill climbs, and often he did very well at them. At one hill-climbing event during a stretch of rainy weather, the hill turned out to be badly waterlogged and the bikes' tires kept slipping in the mud. Burt thought about the situation for a few moments and then borrowed a length of rope, winding it tightly around his rear tyre. One of the other racers laughed that this was the most absurd thing he'd ever seen done to a bike ... but then the race began, and he found himself coming a distant second when Burt scorched up the hill.

Of course, racing had its dangers. Once, when Burt was racing in front of the usual large crowd at the Aspendale Speedway, he made the mistake of glancing down as he gave the bike's oil pump a squeeze. At ninety miles an hour, one glance away from the track was one glance too many. By the time his eyes flicked back to the track, he found himself on a collision course with the murderous post-and-rail fence that ran around the track. He tried desperately to turn. His front wheel hit the deep gutter at the track's edge, the bike leapt into the air and Burt jumped off just before it crashed. Jumping off a bike at ninety miles an hour is not something you do if you have any choice. As he and the bike cartwheeled madly around each other, Burt lost consciousness and woke up a fraction of a second later, still hurtling through the air.

Later he would tell the ambulance men that he clearly remembered blacking out four times as he was cartwheeling. As they lifted him onto a stretcher and carried him to the ambulance room, he was completely dazed. The moment they put the stretcher down he jumped up, insisting he had to go back and finish the race. It took two men to hold him down and he was eventually carted off to hospital, where the doctors told him he had severe bruising and a nasty concussion. He was not allowed out of bed for weeks.

CHAPTER ELEVEN

GOOD FOR PARTS

But there was no keeping Burt away from the racetracks. Before long he and Beryl had moved to Sydney where there was another mile-long speedway course set out in a big D shape. Although it had only opened a couple of years ago the Sydney track attracted a huge number of fans. Some riders became local heroes and were often mobbed by young fans hoping for their autographs. Burt was not quite at this level of fame, but he was one of the better-known riders and he enjoyed the attention he got.

Racing in Australia was really taking off. People were coming to compete from all over the world, bringing their bikes with them. Burt got to know some of the American riders and spent a lot of time looking over their machines. He was getting a name as one of the best mechanics on the racetrack and the other racers often asked him for a hand when their bikes needed a quick-fix or a tune-up. There were other good mechanics around the trackside as well and Burt wasted no opportunity to pick their brains. Most were pleased to answer his questions. He drank it all in, aware that he was in the ideal place at just the right point in history.

For someone with Burt's mechanical genius and love of motorcycles, the Australian speedways in the late 1920s were the best classroom in the world. There are a hundred different ways to bring fuel and air together to make the stream of fire that drives a bike down the home straight. Some are obvious, some are unlikely and some work much better than others. This was the time when Burt learned the deep secrets of the trade. Before long, he could glance at a bike and know exactly what was going on inside it. If you showed him a good new way to solve a bike design problem, Burt would appreciate its beauty the moment he saw it. And he would remember it. The day was going to come when he started putting his new knowledge to work.

But this was not just the moment in history when bike

design first became an art form. It was also the moment of the Great Depression.

People lost their jobs, because no one had the money to pay them their wages. Farmers found no one had the money to buy the food they grew. People went hungry. People lost their homes. Burt found himself out of work.

Suddenly there were no building projects looking for workers, and no one was buying motorbikes, so bike agents had no good reason to loan bikes to racers like Burt. The politicians were busily assuring a panicking world that better times lay just around the corner, but Burt decided he couldn't wait. By now he had two daughters. They needed food every day, not just whenever he could find a few hours' work. There was only one way to provide everything his growing family needed and Burt, swallowing hard, did what he had to do. He booked tickets on a steamer home.

Fate had decreed it was time to get back to farming.

Back at Elston Lea much had changed. Burt's sisters and his little brother Charlie were grown up now, and his mother had begun to take in homeless children. Burt was proud of his mother's good heart, and gave his new foster-brothers and foster-sisters a warm welcome. It was clear, however, that Burt's family could not keep on sharing the old house with this growing number of new siblings, especially once his third daughter was born in 1930. So he decided to take time off from farming to build a new house, almost half a kilometre from his parents' farmhouse.

His two older girls, June and Margaret, often watched him at work in the fields from their bedroom in the old house's attic. It was a happy time for the family, with the five of them getting together for lunch every day on the building site. The house took shape very rapidly. When it was finished it was a comfortable, warm home, with a special display cabinet in the living room to show off all Burt's racing trophies from Australia. His final project was to convert a rickety old hay barn into a proper workshop. With the house finished and his family comfortably installed, he reluctantly turned his attention back to farming.

While he was in Australia the Southland Motorcycle Club had started up. He had – of course – joined it the moment he got back. The club organised rallies, grass-track races, beach racing, cross-country scrambles, hill climbs and socials. The yearly Bluff Hill Climb, a race up a twisty road leading to a local peak, was already very popular with competitors and spectators. Burt was keen to join in, but he no longer had a bike. One day he happened to run into the man who had bought the Indian from him. He asked him how the old bike was doing.

It turned out the man had no idea. He had sold the bike himself, to a chap up in Riverton. Burt decided to track the new owner down.

It took him a few weeks to arrange for someone to give him a lift to Riverton, which was a little town on the coast, but once he was there he soon found his old machine. It looked the worse for wear. Grass was growing up through the wheels and both tires were flat. Obviously no one had ridden it, or even moved it, for some time. It was leaning round the back of the new owner's house, right out in the open. The leather saddle, which had once been so soft and welcoming to sit on, had been fused by the sun and rain into a hard, black lump. The paint had faded. The shiny chrome was pitted with rust. To the casual eye, the machine was a washed-out, lifeless wreck.

Burt's eye was as far from casual as eyes ever get.

He felt a surge of excitement at the sight of the dear old machine. He was almost sure, *almost* sure that he could have it running again very quickly indeed. He took control of himself. It wouldn't do to look too eager. He forced his face into an expression of mild scorn.

'Cripes,' he said to the embarrassed owner, 'this thing looks like it's had it.'

The owner nodded apologetically. 'Yep, she's pretty far gone.'

Burt scratched his head. 'It might be good for parts, I suppose.'

The owner agreed.

Burt thought of a small number and then halved it. The Depression was biting hard and he was pretty sure the man would be happy to get rid of the ruin leaning against his fence. 'I'll give you a pound for it.'

The owner did not even pretend he'd hoped for more. Burt had his bike back.

He went to work right there on the spot. It took about an hour to fix the punctures and get the engine going again. The man who had just sold it to him watched, puzzled. Hadn't Burt said he was going to break the bike down for parts? But the engine ran, as Burt had been sure it would, with the same old sweet, even beat. Burt grinned, and gunned the bike up the road, the back tyre spraying gravel and leaving a cloud of dust in the air. No doubt about it. There were still a few good parts in there.

CHAPTER TWELVE

WHEELS AGAIN

Burt had wheels again. He took to going for long rides on the Indian, roaring over the twisty local roads. He found a wonderful place to practise high-speed jumps, one which none of the other Southland riders had ever thought of using: the front porch of one of the area's small town stores. There was a good big drop at the end of the porch and Burt would sail over it, trying to get further every time. Anyone lucky enough to see him in action was treated to a spectacular show. For the storekeeper, however, it was infuriating. He would be quietly minding his shop, when a great roar would burst in from the porch, followed by a rapid-fire thud-thud-thud-thud-thud as Burt banged his way over the wooden boards. He complained loudly to anyone who would listen that he could never catch the silly bugger and, whoever it was, he was bound to break his neck. But Burt never did. Time after time, the storekeeper would bustle his way from his counter at the back of the shop to the door, planning to give the intruder a piece of his mind. All he ever saw was Burt's behind disappearing around the next corner.

Burt's hot pace also annoyed a few people closer to home. One of the neighbours finally came stomping around to tell Burt that if he continued to spray gravel and dust all over the house every time he went past, he was going to find a length of fencing wire stretched across the road at head height one of these days. Burt took no notice and the man's house continued to wear a grey coat of dust through the summer and a spattering of mud in the winter. Burt Munro slowed down for no one . . . although he did take to ducking down as low as he could when he went past the neighbour's property, just in case the fencing wire threat had not been a joke.

Soon he was racing again. There was a regular grass-track race meeting held at nearby Rugby Park. Burt had told his mates all about the fantastic new cinder tracks he had raced on in Australia, with their loose, sandy surfaces, and about how the riders would drag a foot along the ground to steady the bike as it slid around corners. He was keen to show off the technique, but grass is a very different surface to loose cinders . . . as he soon discovered.

The local newspaper, the *Southland Times*, reported Burt's first race like this: 'Munro provided the thrills in this race. His control of the bicycle as it advanced crab-like was certainly good but after one very prolonged side

Burt and bike.

skid he made a spectacular crash in front of the grandstand. Amidst applause, he immediately remounted and despite further skidding finished the race at good speed.'

He finished dead last, all the same. But the crowd loved him, cheering whenever he stuck his leg out and trailed his foot to throw the bike into a two-wheel slide. They cheered even louder when he bit the dust.

The *Southland Times* soon figured out that Burt was a reporter's dream. Any race he was in was guaranteed to provide a good story, even if the story was about why Burt failed to turn up. In February of 1930, the paper alerted

Racing on Oreti beach in the 1930s. Burt nearest camera.

its readers to Burt's absence from the yearly Bluff Hill Climb: 'H.J. Munro was unfortunate in blowing one of his cylinder heads off, which prevented him from racing throughout the meeting.'

Burt kept working away at his power slides, even in beach races. Sliding was always a tricky job on anything other than a loose surface and the local beaches were hard-packed sand. The only way to make a sliding turn work on them was to get up so much speed that the sand had no choice but to get out of the way, and that was definitely not a technique for the faint-hearted. Most competitors were content to slow down at the markers and simply ride around them. They knew that risking a high speed fall on the beach was not a good idea, because the sand was terribly rough. But if Burt was worried about being flayed alive, he didn't let it change the way he rode. Burt Munro did not slow down. Not even to save his own skin.

It was also an unfortunate truth that braking at high speeds wasn't much of an option for him. In this one area, the Indian was not a well-designed machine. The bike had tiny little brakes that worked fairly well so long as you never went above fifty-five miles an hour and so long as you didn't try using them all that often. Repeated braking at the speeds Burt enjoyed would quickly wear the brakes down to nothing at all, so he tried never to use the bike's brakes if there was a choice. As well as being a great way to show off for the crowds, sliding through the turns let him use the resistance from the sand or grass to slow down a bit.

As the newspaper said after one of his races, 'H. J. Munro can be relied on for a fair turn of speed.'

It wasn't long before all this racing led Burt to his dream job, one that let him get off the farm, support his family and still do all the riding he could ever want. He was about to become a travelling motorcycle salesman.

Gravel road racing in the 1930s.

CHAPTER THIRTEEN

MOTORCYCLE SALESMAN

The Depression had wiped out many jobs in Southland, as it did everywhere. But there was still one thing in this part of the world that an energetic person could fall back on to earn money. They could go after gold.

The goldfields of the New Zealand south had once been among the most productive in the world. Like all such fields, they had lured countless fortune seekers. A few of these men struck huge gold deposits and became rich, but most of them found just barely enough specks and crumbs of the precious metal to pay their living expenses. Some did not even find enough for that. The real money to be made from the New Zealand gold rush lay in selling the gold prospectors food and equipment.

By Burt's time most of the easily won gold was long gone and most of the prospectors had drifted away to other parts of the world, looking for the next big thing. But they had not by any means found all the gold. What was left was just harder to locate. With good paying jobs suddenly so rare, many people decided it might be worth searching for gold along the banks of the wild rivers that had scoured the metal out of the mountains. If you worked hard at it, this could earn you very reasonable amounts of money. It was tough, of course. The region was beautiful in summer, but in the long southern winters it became an icy hell-hole. Only the most determined stuck it out.

These were resourceful people and they had cash. The Tappers motorcycle shop decided it was worth making a major effort to sell a motorcycle to each and every one of them. All they needed was a persuasive salesman who really knew bikes and who was willing to spend time out in the hills finding the prospectors and spinning them enthusiastic tales about all the ways a bike could improve their lives.

Burt was the perfect man for the job. He was a natural salesman who relished the challenge of selling motorcycles to prospectors who probably could not think of anything they needed less. He was not in the least bothered by the need to ride over the appalling roads, which were often just rough tracks carved into the hillsides, with raging rivers far below. If a gold panner protested that the roads were too dangerous for a motorcycle, Burt would simply point out that he had just ridden in on one of them.

Burt's orders were simple. Do whatever it takes to sell the bikes and earn enough to cover your own wages. Slash prices if you have to; offer free crash helmets and saddle bags if it helps make a sale. If anyone even glanced at a machine, Burt offered them a free ride. Whenever he picked up a new machine to sell, Alf Tapper, who owned the shop, would urge him not to bring it back.

Burt as a travelling motorcycle salesman.

Getting home after selling the machine he'd been riding could be tricky. Usually he could get a ride with the new owner, but if the new owner wouldn't leave his diggings, Burt would have to walk back to town. He quite often slept out in the hills and when he did that it usually meant going hungry. Once he got back to the shop he would pick up a new bike and head back home, often pausing for a meal on the way at a little diner in Edendale, where there was a waitress he got on well with. Once, while he was leaving, Burt turned completely around on the saddle to wave goodbye to her and turned back to the road just in time to discover he was heading straight for a train on a level crossing. He instantly threw himself off the bike and skidded into one of the big driving wheels with a solid wallop. Luckily the train was not moving, but Burt was still badly scraped and bruised.

The job was made for Burt, except for two drawbacks. He was often away from his family for weeks at a time and it greatly reduced the time he could spend working on his Indian.

The Indian was ten years old now and she was showing her age. It was hardly surprising. Bike lovers all over the world had spent the last decade doing just what Burt had done in Australia. They had looked at the new designs coming out and swapped ideas on how to make bikes faster and more powerful. These ideas had found their way back to the bike factories. Compared to the new machines that were appearing now, the Indian was like a rabbit trying to outrace a cheetah.

But to Burt she was special. He bought other machines to tune and race from time to time, when he could afford them, but the Indian remained parked securely in his shed long after the others had been forgotten.

To win races on the Indian, however, he needed to increase the bike's power. He set up his shed with all the tools and parts he needed. He built a special ramp, which he could push the bike onto so that he could work on it without bending over. The workshop was no longer just a workshop. It had become a tiny bike factory. Slowly, Burt taught himself to use the new tools.

This was the moment Burt's life changed for ever. He could have kept the Indian in good shape for riding and done his racing on other bikes. But for reasons he only partly understood that was not good enough for him. He wanted to race on the Indian and he wanted to have a shot at winning. The Indian was about to become more than just an Indian. There would soon be as much of Burt Munro in it as there was of its original designers. It was about to become the Munro Special.

Design changes to the Indian.

Burt built his own racetrack on the family farm to let him test the Indian and his other bikes whenever he wanted. His father was still refusing to buy a tractor, so Burt hitched the Clydesdales to the front of a grader and plowed out a quarter-mile oval. The track was a convenient place to develop riding skills and soon a number of Burt's friends were turning up regularly to use it. Burt's father, as always where motorcycles were concerned, did not approve. But he said nothing. He had long ago accepted that his oldest boy would never become a dedicated farmer.

Burt had no way of measuring just how well his changes to the Indian's design were working. He thought he was developing a pretty good sense for when a new idea had improved the bike's performance, but the only real test was to take it out to the beach and see if it went any faster. If it was high tide, or if the beach was blocked by driftwood, he was perfectly happy to use a handy stretch of road called Ryal Bush Straight, just a few kilometres out of town. Other people using the road at these times tended to greet Burt's appearences there with less than perfect joy.

He was now doing well over ninety miles an hour on his fast runs. Most cars and bikes on the roads were lucky to get up to thirty-five. Motorists had no idea Burt was coming from behind until a shattering roar woke them up just in time to see Burt's backside flash past and disappear up the road. If the traffic was coming towards him, the other drivers got even less warning. A small dot would appear in the distance and by the time they had begun to wonder what it was, it had exploded into the foreground and zoomed past them. If there were complaints, Burt never heard them. Not hearing complaints was one of Burt's special talents.

His work on the Indian was producing some real results. He had thought long and hard about the way gas swirled around in the engine as it was compressed on its way to the spark plugs and had decided that the plugs were in the wrong place. He moved them, filling in the old holes with bronze, then drilling new ones. To his delight the change seemed to work.

His chance to put his improvements to the test came in January 1933, the day the Southland Motorcycle Club held a big race meeting on Oreti Beach. The weather was bitterly cold, with a blustery wind blasting in from the Antarctic. Fortunately the rain held off and a large crowd gathered to watch the day's racing. The beach was smoother and harder than it had been for years.

The crowd was kept off the track by heavy ropes. Unfortunately, this was not enough to stop one man wandering onto the course to dig for toheroas, a highly prized shellfish that can be dug up at low tide. He seemed not to notice that the biggest race of the day had started just a few minutes before.

Onlookers watched horrified as the three leading motorcycles bore down on the man. He was bending over with his back to the action, not paying any attention to the shouted warnings. The lead rider veered to the left, missing the man by centimetres at something like one hundred miles an hour. A split second later the second machine, a big 1000cc Indian, screamed past on the man's right.

The third rider was Burt. The two leading bikes had

been between him and the shellfish hunter, stopping him from seeing him until the last moment. The man was now reeling about the beach from the shock of the first two near misses and the spectators could not believe Burt would ever manage to avoid him. Burt jerked the Indian sideways desperately and careered madly on down the beach, skidding out of control for a terrifyingly long moment. The toheroa digger scuttled back to the rope barrier without endangering the rest of the field, which was now streaming past. Someone in the crowd gave him an almighty kick in the pants, to the cheers of all who witnessed it. They then turned back to the furious action on the beach.

Burt had lost a lot of ground avoiding the stray spectator. But the Indian was powering up the track like a train and the second lap saw him close in on the two leaders. When the bigger Indian slowed slightly, Burt slipped past it into second place and held onto it all the way to the end. He earned a useful four pounds prize money.

The second race was the Four Mile Novice Handicap, which of course excluded Burt, who was no novice. But the following Four Mile Open Handicap saw him back on the starting line. He took second place right from the start, with the 1000cc Indian rocketing away to grab a huge lead. Burt was hotly pursued by a number of riders on much newer bikes, but he managed to keep his place and slowly wore the larger Indian's lead down to just twenty yards. It was crowd-pleasing stuff and when he finally crossed the line a split second behind the leader they were cheering him loudly. He happily added another pound to his winnings and prepared for the Six Mile Open Handicap.

Burt blasted off the line in second place again and again held it to the finish, winning another two pounds. He had to miss the last race of the day, because as he crossed the finish line in the Six Mile Open, he had felt something give in his engine. He knew instantly his day's racing was over. He stayed to watch and afterwards had a splendid time talking with his mates, a barbecued sausage wrapped in white bread and smothered in tomato sauce in one hand and a steaming cup of tea in the other. No one cared that the vicious southerly wind was still blasting the beach. It was a great day and it proved that Burt's tuning work had paid off. He was one of the men to beat. The Munro Special was a force to be reckoned with and so was he.

CHAPTER FOURTEEN

BLOWING UP TREE STUMPS

Burt's three girls were now aged between six and ten. They loved hearing him tell stories and he always encouraged them to tell him their own stories from the day. There was never any smacking in the Munro household, or even any shouting. The children had daily chores and they did them without complaint. There was wood to chop, vegetables to be harvested from the garden and dishes to be done. The floors, benches, kitchen table, front step and back step had to be scrubbed regularly and then rinsed with clean water until they were gleaming.

After dinner was often a magic time when the girls were allowed to join their father in the shed. Sometimes

Burt had long curled shavings of metal left over from his work on the Indian. The girls carefully picked up the longest ones and carried them back to the house where they were kept as treasures until a longer piece was found.

As soon as his eldest daughter, June, turned ten, Burt taught her to shoot with his old .22 rifle. She became the first rabbit hunter among his children and the others followed when they were old enough.

There were just two hills in the district, one in town with a water tower on top of it and the other on the Munro property. A stand of macrocarpa trees grew on its gentle top and the girls each chose one to be their own. They learned to climb to the very tops so they could see the distant water tower. They had other hideaways in other places – the bottom of a dry irrigation ditch, or the insides of a hedge.

There was a clear creek close to the farm, swarming with freshwater crayfish. The girls would bait a piece of string with rabbit meat and pull up the creatures, which refused to let go once they had a hold. All the Munro family loved crayfish meat and they would happily sit around a pot of boiling water, eating several pounds of delicious tail meat.

The girls were never more excited than when Burt took

them to blow up tree stumps. Seawood Bush, nearby, had once been a magnificent stand of huge totara trees, but now all that remained were the massive stumps. They would select a stump and Burt would drill a hole in it and drive the heavy log gun deep into place. He would pour a charge of powder into the gun and the girls would be sent to hide behind a carefully chosen log where Burt would join them after lighting the fuse. The blast would tear the stump to pieces, showering the area with chunks of flying wood. They would all be kept busy for several hours chopping up the bigger pieces to fit them in the trailer and collecting the scattered chips for the stove.

In 1935 Burt and Beryl had a son, John. He was a sturdy little fellow and lucky enough to have three doting older sisters, who were the equal of any big brother when it came to showing him how to have fun. It was a wonderful family to grow up in.

Burt was always ready to try anything that might be fun, an approach which led to many family adventures. If heavy rain had created pools in the paddocks, he was the first to encourage his children to swim in them. One very windy year he built a cart with a sail and the children went scooting around the fields. After a rare and memorable snowfall, Burt whipped together a toboggan and took the children for wild rides on it, towing it behind

Burt and his children. L to R: June, Gwen, Burt, Margaret and John.

one of his bikes after wrapping chains around the rear wheel so that it would be safe to use in the snow.

When the Second World War broke out, Burt decided to retrieve his old cannon from his parents' farm. The single shell he had made for it had gone missing, but apart from that he found it pretty much as he had left it. He soon had a new shell ready for use and the whole family gathered one afternoon to watch him fire it. Burt poured in the blasting powder, inserted the shell, then leaned it up against a fence so that it was pointing nearly straight up. With Beryl and the children safely hidden behind a large stump, he lit the fuse and ran to join them. The explosion was satisfyingly loud and Burt was pleased his childhood creation still worked well enough to entertain his own children.

A little while later, Margaret, who had recently started to take John rabbit shooting with her, came across a cow lying dead in a nearby field with a large hole in its back. There was no proof that Burt's cannon had been responsible for the unfortunate beast's death . . . but there was no other likely explanation.

Burt liked nothing better than to throw the children in the family car and motor off to Oreti Beach to hunt for toheroas. But money was always short and in the end he decided to sell the car so he could afford to buy more motorcycles. After that, he had to find other ways of running the family around. He often took his daughters to school on one of the bikes, perching two of them carefully in front of him and one behind. But there was no way this would work for the whole family at once.

A relative who had a beach house at Riverton had offered Burt the use of it. He decided the only way to get the family there was to build a trailer that could be towed behind the bike. He did it and off they went, four little kids sitting in the trailer and Beryl perched on the seat behind Burt. At first all went well, but as Burt became used to the trailer he gradually increased speed. Sadly, the inevitable happened. Sweeping around a bend Burt encountered a deep pile of loose gravel. The trailer overturned and all four children spilled out onto the road. They all suffered minor grazes and were understandably upset. But Burt soon cheered them up and they set off once more. Again Burt gradually increased speed and again the trailer overturned, with the children suffering another lot of bruises and grazes. This time they took longer to cheer up, but they were now over halfway to their destination and there was little choice but to carry on.

The rest of the journey passed uneventfully and the family spent a very happy week playing in the surf and relaxing. To everyone's relief the return trip was slow but steady, with no accidents. In time the children became quite used to the trailer, but it was never their favourite form of transport.

CHAPTER FIFTEEN

FLAT OUT

Burt kept up his efforts in the workshop, to the amusement of his friends. Many of them wondered why he didn't just buy a faster bike instead of trying to turn the Indian into one. He was now making some of his own parts for the bike, which meant heating metal until it melted and pouring it into special moulds. It was a dangerous and sometimes tricky business. A rumour started up at one point that Burt was making parts by going to the beach, lighting a fire, melting a few old pistons in a pot and pouring the molten metal into holes in the sand. The story even made it into the newspapers and Burt enjoyed a quiet chuckle when he read it.

Another time, Burt happened to see a gorse fire raging on a hillside as he was on his way home from work. He had been worrying that the Indian's frame might be developing a few cracks after all the hard riding it had been through and as soon as he spotted the fire he had an idea. He rushed back to his shed at even greater speed than normal, grabbed the bike frame and raced back to the scene of the fire. He hauled the frame through the gorse until he was as close as he could get to the flames and the choking, yellow smoke. After laying down the frame he staggered away from the intense heat, back to the safety of the road.

The following afternoon, once again after work, he retrieved the frame from the now charred hillside, noting with satisfaction that the fire had completely stripped all the oil and paint from it. He had no doubt the heat of the burning gorse had been intense enough to burn away any stress points that might have developed.

The Indian was getting more and more powerful. Some of Burt's improvements turned out to be mistakes and he often had to undo them and start all over again. But as the years went by, the old bike was becoming a real speed machine. The problem with this was that Burt refused to consider improving his brakes to cope with the increase in speed. He wanted all his efforts to be directed at going faster, not slowing down.

The result was that he was beginning to be a danger to

other riders. His riding style made things worse. Although he had amazing skill when it came to controlling his machine, he often made silly mistakes. When he was racing, he would do anything at all if it improved his odds of winning, no matter how reckless or dangerous it might be.

Burt was racing on Oreti Beach one day. He had made a slow start and he was riding hard, trying to make up for it, but he was having trouble closing on the leading rider, a young local named Hew Currie. Hew was a good rider and his bike was more than a match for Burt's Indian. But there was no way Burt was going to be beaten if he could help it. As they approached the second turn during the opening lap, he kept the throttle wide open, planning to skid around the turn at the last possible moment.

Hew took the more sensible approach of slowing down for the turn and Burt crashed straight into him. Even if the Indian had had a decent brake it would have made no difference, because, as everyone watching agreed, Burt was not using the brake anyway.

The impact was terrible. The machines and their riders went cartwheeling down the beach at high speed. When they came to rest Hew was lying motionless on the sand, bleeding from a number of serious wounds. His arms and legs were sticking out at strange angles, as though his bones were broken. Hew's mother, a formidably stout lady, rode out to the accident site with the ambulance, but as soon as she saw her badly injured son she fainted. Mother and son were loaded onto stretchers, a considerable challenge when it came to poor Mrs Currie, and lifted into the ambulance. Then the ambulance men turned their attention to Burt.

He was on his hands and knees looking for his gold teeth, which had been knocked out in the accident. He was not making a great deal of sense and they were worried to see that his crash helmet had been split down the middle. He had obviously taken a major knock to the head. He only agreed to get into the ambulance when his brother Charlie, who had come to watch the racing, promised to take over the search.

Hew Currie took a long time to recover. For some reason Burt was convinced the accident had not been his fault. He often complained bitterly about the loss of his teeth, which Charlie had not managed to find. The Indian was soon repaired and Burt was quickly back in the saddle, racing with his usual lack of restraint. The other riders began to be a little uneasy whenever they saw him at the starting line. Any newcomers going into a race with him were quietly taken aside and warned to be extra careful. 'Burt's always either going flat out or falling off. The problem is, you never know which until it's too late.'

CHAPTER SIXTEEN

FASTEST MAN AROUND

There was one other problem with rebuilding the Indian which Burt had not foreseen. When you make parts of a machine more powerful, you increase the strain on the other parts. It seemed as though every time Burt succeeded in making one bit of the bike work better, another part would promptly break down. All he could do was keep on fixing things whenever they gave way. Sometimes it seemed as though he was moving backwards.

The Indian took up more and more of his time, but he never complained about the setbacks. His son John always remembered watching Burt work for days to produce a particular part for the engine, only to have it break the instant he tested its strength in a vice. He simply removed the broken end from the vice and dropped the two pieces into an old drum he kept for rubbish.

'Better in the vice than in the engine, eh John. We'd rather find out it's a dud right now than later on, wouldn't we?' Picking up another bit of metal, he paused for just a moment. There were days and nights of difficult work ahead of him, all just to make this one part, but he didn't seem bothered by the idea. 'Let's hope this one turns out a bit better!'

Once, Burt took the Indian to a race meeting at Oreti Beach where cars as well as motorcycles were competing. At the end of the day, Burt challenged the fastest car on the beach to a race. The car was given a good head start. It had almost disappeared in the distance before Burt took off after it. The crowd were sure there was no way the old bike would ever catch up and, sure enough, the car was well on its way back down the race course before a tiny dot came into view chasing after it. The dot got larger . . . and larger . . . and, astonishingly, Burt streaked across the finish line a whisker in front of the car. He was going well over 100 miles an hour.

Burt was given a hero's reception. One small boy plucked up the courage to ask a question. 'Mr Munro, what would happen if you opened your mouth when you were going so fast?' Burt considered the question gravely for a moment before replying, 'Why, I suppose it would blow a hole in the back of my trousers.'

It was not long after that that Burt and the Indian set a new land-speed record for New Zealand of 120.8 miles an hour. It was now official. He was the fastest man in the country.

But all was not well with the Munro family. Not long after the war ended in Europe their house burned to the ground. The fire was probably caused by a faulty electricity cable and it destroyed everything they owned. There was nothing for it but to start again and build a new house.

Burt resigned from his motorcycle sales job and threw himself into the building project. The new house was finished in record time. He promptly announced that he was going to move his motorcycles into the front room so he could work on them more easily.

Ever since their time in Australia, Beryl had been unhappy at how much of Burt's energy went into his bikes. He was a good father to his children, but it never seemed there was much time left over for being a good husband. The news that she was going to be sharing her living room with the bikes, coming while she was still reeling from the loss of all her most treasured possessions, was too much for her. She told Burt the marriage was over and moved to Napier, far to the north, taking all the children except Margaret, who chose to stay with her father.

Burt worked at one job or another for a while, but his heart was not in it. He missed the children and none of the jobs had much appeal for him. When Margaret got married a few years later, he was left entirely alone and decided to change his life completely. From now on, he announced to all his friends, he would devote himself entirely to the Indian, working just enough to pay for the food he needed. He would become a fulltime follower of the God of Speed. It seemed to him he had found the perfect way to live.

CHAPTER SEVENTEEN

FASTER STILL

In 1951 Burt bought a small property at 105 Bainfield Road, in north Invercargill, and went to the council for permission to build a new house. At the time the council had a rule that house ceilings should be no less than eight feet high. Burt thought this was ridiculous. A higher ceiling meant it would be harder to keep the house warm. He asked permission to build with a ceiling height of seven feet. The council did not see why their rules should be bent for Burt's convenience, and turned down his request.

Burt thought for a while and then announced he would build a large garage before embarking on the house. The garage would have a ceiling height of seven feet, but that was all right because rules for garages were a lot more flexible than for houses. Soon, however, the council noticed that Burt, having finished the garage, did not seem to be in any great hurry to go to work on the house. In fact he seemed to be living in the garage. Inspectors began to call, asking when Burt was planning to begin building his proper home. Burt always showed them a few lines on a piece of paper he had stuck up on the wall. This, he said, was the beginning of a drawing to help him decide exactly what style of dwelling he wanted. As soon as he had made up his mind, he would build the new house. Of course he was not planning on staying in the garage. That would be against the law!

Burt stayed in that garage for another twenty-eight years.

He wasted little time setting up his new home – as he privately thought of the garage – to suit his needs. A single bed rested across the end wall, with a couple of old suitcases underneath, containing all his clothes. Shelves ran the length of one long wall and a workbench went against the other. His special motorcycle stand went in the middle of the room and a small stove sat just inside with its chimney sticking out through the double doors. The gutters fed rainwater into a wooden barrel, which Burt used for cooling hot metal and also for making tea. There was one small window facing north.

Every now and again he would cook a load of sausages in a frying pan, eating a few and chucking the pan back on the stove when he felt hungry again. Visitors were almost always welcome. He would drag a chair out and carefully drape it with a sheet of clean newspaper to keep their clothes from getting grubby. Then he'd serve them a cup of tea, which tasted strangely of metal, and some gingernut biscuits. The local children quickly discovered they could always score a biscuit from him and he was happy to tell them about what he was doing. Many of them found his activities interesting and visited regularly.

One new visitor was a young builder called Russell Wright, who was as keen on high-speed racing as Burt was. He liked nothing better than to talk with Burt about tuning bikes for better speed.

By now the Indian had been taken to pieces and rebuilt many times over. Soon after moving into the garage, Burt reached a new top speed, taking the Indian up to a quite remarkable 133 miles per hour during a speed trial. Many people thought Burt had finally stretched the Indian as far as it would go. But Burt thought otherwise. He was determined to go a heck of a lot faster yet. Burt was putting in sixteen hours' work on the Indian most days now, knocking off late at night and rising again after just a few hours' sleep. He did not stop for weekends or holidays, and even on Christmas Day he gave himself only a half-day off.

But he still welcomed interruptions from people whose company he enjoyed and one day he was pleased to see Russell Wright striding up the narrow path through the long, straggly grass. Russell had just bought a brand new Vincent Black Lightning. It had taken twelve months for the bike to arrive from overseas, but it was well worth the wait. It was a beautiful piece of engine design and it impressed Burt enormously.

The heart of the Munro Special in its final form.

Naturally Burt wanted to know what she was capable of, and Russell was equally keen to find out. The pair set off for the beach. At 100 miles an hour Russell discovered something Vincent owners the world over were beginning to find out – they had a strange and unpredictable habit of suddenly getting out of control. Afterwards, Russell could not remember if he hit a small bump or a soft patch of sand, but he vividly remembered nearly being thrown off the bike. It was only with great difficulty that he hung on and slowed without crashing. He and Burt had a long hard look over the bike but could find no obvious explanation for its behaviour. In the end, Burt came out with a classic piece of Burt Munro advice: 'The problem might go away at higher speed. Next time try opening the throttle instead of closing it.'

Six months later Russell took the Vincent to a speed trial held on Tram Road, an arrow-straight byway. He was hoping for the New Zealand motorcycle speed record. Russell roared along the road, quickly getting the bike up to over 180 miles an hour. The machine ran steady as a rock and he found it easy to stay bang in the middle of the six-metre-wide road . . . until he flashed past a hole in one of the roadside hedges and discovered there was a tiny breeze blowing through the hedge. At 185 miles an hour, that tiny breeze felt like someone taking a sledgehammer to one of Russell's wheels. The bike began to wobble and for a moment he was sure he was about to crash. Somehow he finished the run, but his face was white as ash as he climbed shakily out of the shell. There and then he swore he would never try speeds like that on a road course again. But he had done the job. The record was his at 185.15 miles an hour.

When Russell called around to tell Burt about the record, he found him working away as usual on the Indian. Burt was delighted with Russell's achievement and he was was particularly interested in the part about the crosswind nearly running him off the road and killing him.

He made a cup of tea and passed the tin of gingernuts. Russell dunked one in his cup. They both sat in comfortable silence for a moment before Burt spoke again. 'So, are you going to have another go?'

Russell hesitated. 'I might. But not here. It's too bloody dangerous.'

'Utah then,' suggested Burt.

Russell nodded. 'Yep, the salt's the place for speed.'

Burt drained his tea. 'Well, if you do go would you mind if I tagged along? I'm thinking of taking my old girl over some time and I'd like to check things out there first. I'll pay my own way and I'd make myself useful.'

Russell looked up in surprise. His eyes swept around the shed, taking in the faded, battle-scarred Indian.

'You can come if you like,' he said, smiling. 'But you'll have to make the tea.'

CHAPTER EIGHTEEN

FIRST TRIP TO THE SALT

Burt knew Russell was right. Utah was the place to go for speed and it was also the place Burt could learn some things he needed to know. As Russell's near-disaster with the crosswind showed, part of the secret of high-speed racing is to get the air to flow smoothly over your bike. The faster you go, the more problems air resistance can give you. What the Indian needed more than anything else was a streamliner body. If Burt could build an outer shell that would cover all of the bike except the very bottoms of the tires, then hunker down inside the shell himself, they would slide through the air like a fish sliding through water.

But he needed to know a lot more about streamlining before he could design a shell that would do the job. By following Russell to Utah, he would gain the chance to see how other racers streamlined their bikes.

He was packing for the trip when he heard his neighbour sing out to him. 'I hear you're going away, Burt. How about mowing the lawn before you go? It's a bloody disgrace. I'll lend you my mower. There's even a can of petrol to fill it up.'

Burt looked at the grass. His neighbour had a point. It came up to his waist. Bit of a job for a lawnmower . . . Later that day he walked next door and inspected the lawn mower and the can of petrol. He wet his finger and held it in the air to confirm there was a gentle breeze blowing towards the road. Then he picked up the can of petrol.

By the time the fire brigade arrived the long grass in front of Burt's shed was reduced to smoking stubble. Burt was most apologetic. He explained he had had no idea the fire would be so spectacular and promised not to do it again. As the fire engines left Bainfield Road with a couple of final toots on their horns, Burt surveyed his handiwork with satisfaction. No one could say his grass was too long now.

One long boat ride, one quick plane flight and one substantial bus trip later, Burt was in Wendover, a small town on the edge of the great Utah salt flats. He was immediately at home. The place hummed with activity, nearly all of it focused on making machines of different kinds go faster than they ever had before. There were big professional outfits like the NSU team, which arrived with various machines and a party of thirty, including timing technicians, mechanics, team managers and riders. There were smaller teams, most of them folk like Burt, with next to no money and vast amounts of enthusiasm. These were exactly Burt's kind of people. He soon began to make friends.

From the moment he saw the salt flats, Burt loved them. Under the fierce sun they glittered a pure, burning white, stretching away as flat as concrete to the low purple hills on the horizon. During the day the mirage of an island shimmered in the middle distance and sometimes a phantom lake formed. Sunsets were spectacular, with the flats seeming to catch alight against a fiery red and gold sky. It was a place made for magic.

The area used for record attempts had a hard salt crust at least fifteen centimetres deep. It was about twenty-four kilometres long and sixteen wide. A huge plane of thinner salt surrounded it, with thick mud trapped just below its surface. This thinner salt crust was only four millimetres deep in some places and any vehicle foolish enough to stray onto it was likely to find itself sinking into a mud wallow very quickly indeed.

Humans had generally avoided the area in earlier times, because salt in large quantities is a very effective poison. Nothing would grow on the flats and no animals could live there. Native Americans had found no use for the place and early wagon trains of European settlers had learned the hard way how risky crossing the thin salt could be. Several had come close to meeting an unpleasant end. But early in the twentieth century a Utah businessman came up with the idea of racing cars on the salt. The hard, perfectly flat surface turned out to be ideal for high-speed racing. As people built faster

Sir Malcolm Campbell's Bluebird.

and faster machines, it began to become apparent that there were not many places in the world where you could go extremely fast for very long without crashing into something. The salt became more and more popular.

One of the first people to try for the land-speed record on the salt was Sir Malcolm Campbell, who arrived from England in 1937 with a specially built Rolls-Royce, a streamlined car he called Bluebird. Bluebird had bellowed across the flats to break the 300-mile-an-hour mark for the first time in history. From then on all land-speed records had been set there. Every year since 1947, a group called the Southern California Timing Association ran an event called Speed Week, where anyone could come and have their speed measured with scientific accuracy.

Burt arrived at the salt a month or so before Speed Week, but there was already plenty going on. The German NSU team was there, preparing two of their machines for an assault on the records. One of these bikes was a perfect teardrop shape with a long tail. The rider was completely enclosed and peered out through a curved Plexiglas screen set into the nose. The second bike was even more unusual, with the driver lying back in a hammock inside, barely above the ground. The thing was like a tiny missile on wheels.

The German NSU team had unusual bikes. This is the Baumm hammock.

Rain caused problems for a few days, but as soon as the salt dried the Germans went to work. There was a moment of unplanned excitement when the teardrop bike hit a patch of still-damp salt at very high speed. It veered off-course, demolishing one of the timing lights on the side of the course, but no one was hurt.

The rules for the speed trials were very strict. In order to set an official world record, it was not enough to get up to the required speed once. To make timing errors less likely, racers had to run the course twice, after which their times were added together and divided by two. There were

The NSU team's Delphin bike.

different records for different classes of bike, but the big
one was the overall motorcycle speed record and Burt was
right on the spot when that one fell. He had persuaded
one of the officials to let him sit with them and so he had
a ringside seat as one of the German bikes blazed its way
to a two-way average of 210.64 miles an hour, the fastest
time any bike had ever recorded, anywhere in the world.

After that it was almost dull to see his friend Russell
achieve a 198-mile-an-hour average. It was a real accom-
plishment but, compared to the Germans, Russell was like
a tall man standing next to a giant.

Seeing Russell's run was what he had come over for, but Burt was now determined to stay on for Speed Week. There was a slight problem with that, because his entry visa to the United States was due to expire, meaning it was against the law for him to stay in the country any longer on this trip. But Burt took his usual approach to other people's rules, which was to ignore them. He decided to forget the visa extension and stay anyway – a decision he would never regret. It allowed him to meet a number of fellow worshippers at the altar of the God of Speed. Many of them became his lifelong friends.

Among them was a short, powerfully built fellow called Marty Dickerson, a man famous for setting a number of records on Vincent motorcycles. Marty had turned up to watch the NSU team in action and, like Burt, stayed for Speed Week. The year before he had ridden a supercharged Vincent Black Lightning bike across the salt at a blazing 177 miles an hour, setting a new record for the fastest non-streamlined bike.

Burt's open and friendly manner combined with his tales of impossible speeds on an old Indian Scout soon intrigued Marty. Russell was still around and he soon confirmed that Burt's stories were true. He really had ridden a 1920 Scout at over 130 miles an hour.

At the end of Speed Week, when all the bikes and other

vehicles had had their turn and done their best, Burt asked Marty if he could catch a ride with him and his wife back to Los Angeles. He was short of cash after flying in and he wanted to make the little money he had left last as long as possible. Marty was happy to help, but he only had a small truck and he had already agreed to take another passenger. He was very sorry, but with three in the cab the only place Burt could ride would be on the back.

Burt's face lit up at the suggestion and he assured Marty that this arrangement would be perfect. Marty explained that he would be driving non-stop, a distance of about 1200 kilometres, with pauses only for food and petrol. This just made Burt beam even more. There was no point in dawdling; a straight run was just the ticket! There seemed little left to discuss and Marty helped Burt clear a space out of the wind. As they headed on to the highway Marty looked in the rear-view mirror to check on Burt and saw him leaning back comfortably, hair ruffled gently by the breeze, as he gazed at the landscape sliding by. For a moment Marty thought Burt was shouting at something. Then he heard the faint strain of an old song above the noise of the wind. Burt Munro was singing.

CHAPTER NINETEEN

THE STREAMLINER

Burt caught a boat home from Los Angeles. It was a pleasant sea voyage and he arrived back in New Zealand feeling relaxed and ready for work. There was a great deal to do. His travels had opened his eyes to new ideas and possibilities. He was going to give the Indian more speed than she'd ever had and then he was taking her to Utah.

He threw himself into the job. He was in the workshop morning to night, sometimes barely remembering to eat. It was a good thing for him he had loyal friends, who went out of their way to keep a kindly eye on him, often arriving for a visit armed with a great pile of steaming fish and chips wrapped in newspaper. Many of these friends were motorcycle enthusiasts too. One of them, Duncan Meikle, was as stubborn and full of ideas as Burt was. The two could have some terrible arguments, usually after Burt had said or done something Duncan found completely outrageous. One thing that really annoyed Duncan was Burt's habit of accelerating the instant his bike started. The problem was that Duncan would usually be giving him a push at the time and would end up stretched out full length, face down on the ground. No matter how many times he yelled and swore at Burt for doing it, and no matter how many times Burt promised not to do it again, he always did. The quarrels never lasted long.

Once, Burt and Duncan were in Burt's workshop, working on another old bike of Burt's, a Velocette. Burt suspected the back wheel was buckled and wanted to check it, so he raised the machine on a block of wood, leaving the back wheel free to spin a few centimetres off the floor. Duncan kneeled behind the machine and started it up and Burt, at the other end, slipped it into top gear. He revved the engine as hard as he could – the faster the wheel turned, the easier it would be to spot any telltale wobbles. But as soon as he revved the engine, the machine jumped off the block, spinning its wheel furiously on the floor. Burt just managed to grab the front brake.

As the shed began to fill with tyre smoke, Burt made

the mistake of shutting the throttle. The tyre slowed, of course, but on the slippery lino it was actually easier for it to get good traction at this lower speed. The bike rocketed forward, zooming round and round in a circle with Burt in the middle, desperately hanging on, and Duncan staying well back out of the way. Slowly the bike's circular path edged closer to the side of the room and Burt found himself dragged underneath the cluttered, all-purpose table. There was a tremendous crash and suddenly pots and pans were showering down everywhere, while the engine kept booming away and the back wheel kept spinning, occasionally finding traction again and throwing everything back in the air. Finally, Duncan managed to reach in and switch off the bike. He dragged it out from the wreckage to free Burt, who was miraculously unhurt. The two men looked at each other blankly for a few seconds and then laughed. Burt recovered his breath enough to ask Duncan if the wheel was in fact buckled.

Duncan shrugged. 'Hell man, d'ya seriously expect me to notice with all that going on?'

Burt snorted. 'Well of course I do. You could see I was busy!'

But Burt's main task during this period was to give the Indian its streamlined outer shell. Burt had thought long and hard about streamlining, mulling over everything he had seen in the United States. He had come to the conclusion that rather than fitting a high teardrop shape onto a standard bike frame as most record-breakers had up until that point, it would be more sensible to lower the bike as much possible. This would reduce the flow of air under the machine and also, he hoped, make it sturdier when dealing with crosswinds.

He now knew from his time on the salt flats that the breezes there could come from any direction. It was not unusual for a racer to encounter several puffs from several different angles during a speed run. But for the Indian to support the long, low, streamlined body he wanted to make, the bones of the machine would have to be longer and stronger. He was going to have to rebuild its frame.

Walking through the botanical gardens in Invercargill one fine afternoon he stopped to enjoy a moment in the sun by the big ornamental goldfish pond. The fish were swimming lazily to and fro. Suddenly something startled them and in an instant they flashed the length of the pond and took shelter under a waterlily. The way they moved! Burt was thunderstruck. To slip through the water so quickly, they must possess the perfect streamlined shape. If he could give the Indian a shape like that . . .

He returned to that park a number of times to study

and sketch the fish. This was unusual behaviour for Burt. Normally he made bike parts, and often quite complex ones, without ever making plans in advance. But he was eager to capture the goldfish shape as precisely as possible and detailed sketches were the only way to achieve that.

He set about hacking and altering the frame of the Indian to make it 60 inches longer and as low to the ground as possible. He cut, sawed, drilled, making everything as snug as he could get it. No wasted space and no extra weight. The more weight you carried, the slower you'd go. Anything that could be shaved was shaved.

Burt wearing his standard beach racing gear.

Everything that could be junked was junked. By the time he'd finished, the bike had lost about half its weight.

A couple of months later, the streamlined shell was still not fitted, but everything else on the Indian was ready. Burt and Duncan took it to the Pioneer Motorcycle Club speed trials to have a crack at the New Zealand speed record for the 750cc class.

The adventure was almost over before it started. They took the bike for a quick safety check, as you always had to before a speed trial. The safety scrutineer took one look at Burt's tires and told Burt that he could not possibly run.

Up until the fifties Burt had used beaded wheels – an older type of tyre absolutely unsuitable for high-speed runs. At very high speeds, the outer rubber layer of a tyre tries to pull away from the wheel and needs to be held securely in place. Beaded wheels were not designed to cope with this problem and Burt had been lucky to get away with using them for so long. But recently he had switched to road-racing tyres, which were still far from ideal for the speeds he was achieving. The problem with these newer ones was their tread, the pattern of little bumps in the rubber designed to help the tyres grip the road. At Burt's speeds, those little bumps hit the road with the force of big bumps, the same way little cross-breezes began to feel like gale-force winds. Burt had a simple solution to this. He cut the tread off. Unfortunately he sometimes cut just a little too deep and left patches of tire with no rubber on them at all. The speed-trial scrutineer pointed at just such a patch and told Burt he could not run.

Burt fixed the scrutineer with a look of cold determination. 'If I'm game to run on them, what's your damn problem?'

The official looked at the patch of canvas and then back at Burt. He was clearly confronted with a much stronger will than his own. In the end he relented. As he said later, 'The old bugger's been riding on tyres like that for years. Who was I to tell him he had to change his ways?'

Burt took the bike down to the track and proceeded to set a new record: an astonishing 143.58 miles an hour. This was a stunning achievement. Many people might have considered it a fitting climax to thirty-seven years' dedicated racing. Many people would have promptly retired, convinced they would never do better.

Burt went straight back home and got to work on the streamliner.

CHAPTER TWENTY

ONE GOOD RUN

Burt made several more trips to Utah before he was ready to take the Indian there. It drove him mad with frustration to stand on the sidelines and watch other people race, especially when he was sure the Indian could beat most of them, if only he had the streamlining finished. But it was a major job and there was nothing to be gained by doing it too quickly and getting it wrong.

He took the opportunity to see more of the United States during these trips. On one occasion, he found his way to Springfield, Massachusetts – the home of the Indian Motorcycle Company.

The company had fallen on hard times since the 1920s. By the time Burt paid his visit, the factory was largely empty. But there was life in the place still, as he soon discovered. Wandering around the vast brick structures he came across a collection of cars parked near an open roller door. From the door he saw a number of men working under the beams of massive overhead floodlights. Racks of shelving stretched away into the gloom. He shouted out a greeting, his voice echoing in the huge space, and one of the men walked briskly over to investigate. Burt explained who he was in his usual forthright manner and was invited inside. To his astonishment he found the shelves sagging under the weight of hundreds of tonnes of Indian spare parts. The spare-parts department was the one part of the factory still thriving and the men who worked there were kept busy supplying orders. Pistons, crankshafts, bodywork, brake shoes, headlights – the list went on and on.

It was not long before everyone had gathered to hear Burt's story, which he willingly told. He had no money to spare, but when he finally left hours later he had a new crankpin and enough bearing rollers in his pocket to keep him going for years. He had also made a number of friends who would from that day follow his achievements with a renewed sense of pride, friends he would make a point of keeping in touch with. The Indian Motorcycle Company might be down on its luck, but with people like Burt about it could never be dead.

Burt had now spent five long years hammering the Indian's streamliner case into shape. The hand-beaten aluminium was strong enough to hold together at high speed, but thin enough that it added very little to the bike's weight. It had exactly the goldfish shape Burt had aimed for and every inch of its surface was covered in tiny

Burt squeezed into the first streamliner body.

dents from Burt's hammer, which looked a little like fish scales from a distance. Three little fins at the rear gave it added stability – or at least that was the plan. Until Burt raced the bike at high speed, there was no way to tell if his goldfish design worked.

It was a big day for Burt when he took his streamlined Indian to the 1960 Canterbury speed trials for its first real test. Five years' hard work. Had he got it right, or was he going to have to start again?

His first attempted run revealed a terrible error. He had concentrated so hard on copying the goldfish shape as precisely as possible that he had made the body too narrow. Crouching inside the shell in his workshop, all had seemed fine, but it was a different matter on the road. The cramped cockpit prevented him from shifting his weight to control the bike. In fact, it was so tight he could hardly get his hand down to the gear lever.

He made a run anyway and somehow got the bike up to 161.75 miles an hour. It was a frightening experience. The machine became airborne whenever it hit a bump. On the return run, at something approaching 150 miles an hour, the mainshaft broke on the drive side of the engine and the bike skidded straight down the road for 150 metres. How he kept it on two wheels, given the way he was stuffed rigidly into the cockpit, he could never afterwards explain. It was his most terrifying escape yet. He was badly shaken by the experience, openly admitting how horrible it had felt as the bike slid on and on, constantly on the brink of crashing. He made only a couple of extra test runs before concluding the shell was useless and, worse, dangerous. After countless hours of work over five years, he would have to make a new one.

But there was a way to speed up the process. He could make the useless shell into a mould and use it to make a fibreglass replacement. Fibreglass was a lighter material and easy to work with.

He smothered the old shell with a special releasing agent, so that the fibreglass would not stick to the aluminium once it had set, and began brushing on coats of a fuming, sticky substance called epoxy resin. When it set, this would become fibreglass. Someone had told him the right temperature for the process was twenty-one degrees Celsius, so he stoked up the potbelly and soon had the shed swelteringly hot. How Burt handled such hellish conditions day after day was something his friends could never understand.

The new shell was finally ready and it looked good, if a little rough. Burt finished it off with a quick coat of red paint – Indian Red, naturally.

Burt had already decided against another test run in

New Zealand. He needed space, lots and lots of space. He had no ambitions to break records or win fame. He knew that even if he did break records, he would not win fortune. He wanted to go to the salt for one very simple reason: he had put all his effort into building the machine and now he wanted to find out just how fast it could go. He asked for nothing more than one good run, just one time when the God of Speed would smile down upon him and grant him the luck to run down the salt track and back without anything going wrong.

He booked space on the freight ship *Cap Ortega* and set about making a crate for the bike and its trailer. He would travel by passenger ship, arriving in Los Angeles in time to buy an old car, and then drive up the coast to San Francisco in time to meet the *Cap Ortega*, load up the Indian and tow it 1000 kilometres to Bonneville.

It was a good plan. There was no way Burt could know it was going to go dreadfully wrong.

CHAPTER TWENTY-ONE

A DATE AT BONNEVILLE

Burt's ship, the *Pacific Star*, barely qualified as an ocean liner. It offered only a few small cabins for its handful of passengers. But it was luxury compared with his workshop home. Burt leaned happily on the rail and watched the pale blue coast of New Zealand slowly merge with the low cloud stretching along the horizon. Aotearoa, Maori called the country, land of the long white cloud, and now he knew why. He felt the faint trembling of the deck beneath his feet whenever the ship shouldered a wave. He was on his way.

For the first few days he enjoyed mooching about, reading all the paperback Westerns that jammed the shelves in the ship's little lounge. By the fourth day he was impatient and beginning to wonder if he should have found the money for an airfare. The captain's table, where officers and passengers dined, provided Burt with a willing audience for his tales of high and low adventure in the pursuit of speed. But he was not used to having nothing to do. Strangely, he found the idleness very tiring. As the west coast of the United States loomed ahead, time seemed to go slower and slower. He began to fear the ship would never arrive.

When it finally did, the captain shook his hand solemnly, wishing him the best in his speed attempts and telling him to take care. Burt smiled at that. When you ventured into the realm of the God of Speed, its lord might smile on you or he might not. All the care in the world would make no difference. Crew and passengers wished him well as he lugged his suitcase down to the dock. And then, after a final cheery wave, he was alone again.

The sun bouncing off the dock's old metal warehouses was so bright that his eyes hurt. Shading his face with his spare hand, he lugged his battered suitcase all the way from the customs shed to the bus stop. Burt Munro did not use taxis; he had no money for them. After an hour's wait in the heat, a tired old bus came grinding along and he was on his way to Los Angeles. He was almost the only passenger and he settled in the seat opposite the driver, an elderly black man. The breeze through the open window revived him and he turned to the driver for a chat.

His first attempt was met with a series of wary glances, but when Burt explained he had just stepped off a boat from New Zealand the driver warmed. He had been to New Zealand during the war. When Burt told him his plans he became even more enthusiastic. He had a friend who had ridden Indian motorcycles and insisted they were the best machines in the world. How fast did Burt hope to go on this particular Indian?

'Two hundred miles an hour.'

'Man, you must be some kind of crazy!'

The old couple at the back, curious to know more, shuffled forward and joined in. Like the driver, it turned out they had once had a friend who rode an Indian. They too expressed amazement at Burt's ambitions. None doubted for a moment, however, that Burt was telling the truth or that he fully intended to go through with his plan.

The road along the coast swung inland through miles of housing, and then emerged onto a busy road with car yards on either side as far as Burt could see. This was the place for him. He picked up his suitcase and got off the bus. Most of the cars for sale were far too modern and expensive. It took another hour of trudging from sale yard to sale yard for him to find a likely target.

It was a 1940 Nash, a cheap car even when it was new, and now something of a wreck. Every panel carried at least one major dent and the black paintwork was peeling like sunburnt skin. But the car seemed rust-free, and better yet it had a tow bar he could attach the Indian's trailer to. He peered at the price label. $80! Far too much. Burt reluctantly turned away, only to find his way blocked by a salesman. He introduced himself as Pete of Pete's Auto Emporium. He had seen Burt admiring the old beauty and wondered if he might like a closer look.

'They don't make them like that anymore,' he assured Burt, smiling at the old humpbacked heap. 'And Lord knows it's cheap!'

Burt climbed into the driver's seat and Pete pointed out the original radio. He said it actually worked – along with everything else except the gas gauge, which always read empty, and the inside light. And the windscreen wipers only worked when the car had warmed up. Burt fiddled with the key, trying to get the car to start. After half a minute he was about to give up when to his surprise it suddenly roared to life. He could tell it was running on four of its six cylinders at most and it was blowing a lot of smoke.

Equally surprisingly, it seemed Pete was telling the truth about the windscreen wipers and the radio, both of which did work, though not very well. Burt left the car running and climbed out to inspect it, at which point the engine coughed and died.

An inner voice was telling him he should leave, but Pete was right behind him talking about what a great car this was and Burt was finding it hard to turn away. In desperation he offered the man $50, which was the most he could afford. He was sure he would be turned down. Sure enough, Pete shook his head and looked disappointed. Burt quickly shook hands with the salesman, wished him a good afternoon and headed for the street.

Pete called after Burt's retreating back that $50 would be fine if that was all he had. Burt thought a moment. 'I'll take it,' he said, 'if you can lend me a tool box for a few minutes.'

Burt took the few tools Pete could find and dived under the hood of the Nash, humming as he worked. Pete stuck around, curious to see what Burt might achieve with such crude equipment. When Burt asked him to hop in and turn the key, he was very surprised to hear the car start on all six cylinders. Burt continued to fiddle and within a few moments the engine had settled to a steady even beat. It had also stopped smoking. Pete was both annoyed and impressed.

'Mister, you really know your way around cars, don't you? I could do with a man like you around here.'

Burt shook his head. 'Sorry Pete, I've got a date at Bonneville.'

Burt drove up the road to a gas station and filled the car up, grinning when he paid the attendant. Petrol was so cheap here!

With the car problem solved, he finally allowed himself to rejoice in the pleasure of being back in the country he had come to love. Americans were expansive, friendly people who would open up and talk to you with just the slightest encouragement. It was the home of 'can do' and 'no trouble at all', the land of cheap gas and cheap cars. He patted the Nash on its bulbous nose. How bad can you be? he thought. You were made here.

He bought a map of the city and asked the attendant about the best route to Marty Dickerson's home – a considerable distance involving a number of different freeways. Although he had made the journey a number of times, it was easy to get hopelessly lost. He thought of phoning Marty to tell him he had arrived but decided not to. If Marty was not home he would wait. He had nowhere else to go. He had just enough money to get to Utah and back, so long as he dealt with any problems himself or got help from the kindred spirits he always seemed to meet when he needed them.

Marty was one such spirit. When he opened the door to see Burt climbing out of the car, he grinned delightedly and positively skipped down the front path, pumping Burt's hand and patting his back. 'It's fine to see you, Burt. But why the hell didn't you call when you arrived?' His eyes swept over the battered old Nash and he could not suppress a grimace. 'Gee Burt, you sure know how to pick 'em.'

In the cool late afternoon, Burt took Marty's tools and

Burt, Jackie and Marty Dickerson at home in Los Angeles.

hammered the worst of the dents out of the old car. He made a more than decent job of it. When Marty suggested they buy a tin of black paint to finish the job, Burt shook his head – he had no money for paint. Besides, it wouldn't make the Nash go any better, would it?

They went inside for a cold beer – Burt had a cup of tea – while Marty and his wife, Jackie, prepared steaks for the barbecue. Inevitably, the conversation turned to setting speed records. They talked about the way things had changed, as they always do, with the passing years.

When Burt first went to Speed Week, it had been a fairly relaxed event. Back then you could lie stretched out on a motorcycle with your legs trailing out behind, wearing nothing but a pair of swimming togs, and open out the throttle. But that was then.

Now most people seemed to think you needed flame-proof clothing, parachutes and all manner of special equipment. It was a different game, even if these things were not yet compulsory. Burt thought of his ancient, worn sandshoes, the only footwear he ever wore for record attempts, and felt worried for a moment. All he wanted, all he had ever wanted, was one good run, one chance to see what his life's work had produced. Listening to Marty and Jackie, he wondered if the Speed Week people would really let him have his chance.

He shrugged off his doubts and relaxed. He was in the company of fellow worshippers of the God of Speed and he was back in the United States, a country that had surely been made for people like him. He was here and right now that was all that mattered.

As the next day dawned, just as bright and sunny as the last, Burt was already busy, tearing the rear seat out of the Nash. Marty had found an old single mattress and, with the back seat gone, there was just enough room for it. He now had a perfectly comfortable mobile bedroom. Time to head up to San Francisco to pick up the bike and trailer. There would be showers and toilets at many of the gas stations along the way. Burt was confident his journey would be a comfortable, relaxed affair.

He should have known better.

He was so busy waving goodbye to his friends that he forgot for a moment that Americans, unlike New Zealanders, drive on the right side of the road, not the left. He confidently set off straight into the oncoming traffic. Marty and Jackie yelled warnings, which Burt mistook for enthusiastic farewells. He did notice vaguely that there seemed to be a car heading in his direction. What did its driver think he was doing? You got some real fools on the road sometimes. He revved the Nash's engine and waited confidently for the idiot to get out of his way.

At the last moment he realised that he was the one in the wrong. He spun the wheel desperately and missed the other car by slightly more than a layer of paint. It was hard to say who was more shocked, Burt or the two ladies he'd almost killed. They all stopped and got out of their cars and Burt apologised at great length, explaining the reason for his lapse and begging their forgiveness. After ensuring no harm had been done he set off once again, this time on the right side of the road.

Four hours later he was still driving around in circles looking for the road north. In his agitation he drove through a red light and was pulled over by a highway patrol car. Burt climbed out of the Nash and greeted the patrolman by shaking his hand, introducing himself as Burt Munro from New Zealand and asking politely how he could be of assistance. The cop was taken aback. He was not used to people being so friendly when he was about to give them a ticket. He told Burt sternly that failing to stop for a stop sign was a matter of the utmost seriousness. Burt agreed wholeheartedly, but explained he had been trying to find the signs pointing the way north. If only, he complained, those signs were a little easier to spot, then a man would not be distracted from seeing even more important signs. It was downright dangerous.

The patrolman conceded that Burt had a point. But had Burt noticed his car's tail-lights were not working? Burt was shocked. Not working? Why, he had checked them himself not half an hour before and they had been just fine. He assured the officer he would have them checked immediately. Imagine driving in a place like the United States without tail-lights. It didn't bear thinking about. It was about as dangerous, he guessed, as doing two hundred miles an hour on a 1920 Indian motorcycle on the Bonneville salt flats.

The patrolman looked at the elderly tourist with fresh interest. Was Burt really planning to compete at Speed Week? Burt launched into his story. It was a good twenty minutes before he stopped to draw breath, by which time any thoughts the patrolman had of giving him a ticket were forgotten. That had been Burt's plan. He turned the conversation back to the way north and was given clear directions. Burt shook the man's hand again and climbed back into the Nash, finally able to relax. Paying for running a stoplight was definitely not something he had counted on when he set his budget.

Burt hated driving at night. He was soon parked up outside a cosy diner, where he enjoyed a hearty meal of steak and fries. Soon enough he was safely snoring in the back of the Nash, sleeping soundly as the big trucks rumbled past. In the morning, after he had showered at the gas station across the road, a new shift of waitresses took his breakfast order. Not long after first light he was on his way again. By mid-afternoon, he had made it to the docks in San Francisco, only to learn that his ship had been delayed and would not reach port for another sixteen days. There was no way Burt could make it to the salt flats in time for Speed Week.

CHAPTER TWENTY-TWO

A CHANGE OF PLANS

For a moment Burt almost gave way to despair. But he asked a few more questions and soon learned that the ship would be docking in Seattle, 1350 kilometres further north, before sailing on to San Francisco. If he could unload his bike and trailer there he could just make it to Bonneville in time.

Roughly half a minute later, Burt was back on the road. Another man might have been bothered by having his careful plans disrupted, but Burt quickly decided his new plan was even better than the old one. It would let him see even more of the United States!

A day later he was making his way up into the

foothills of the Cascade Mountains. Once he was over the mountain range, it would be an easy drive to Seattle. He had expected the ascent to be hard work for the old car, but it was a smooth, easy climb. As he breasted the last sharp ridge he gave a sigh of relief, and began the long descent toward his destination.

But the road on this side of the mountain seemed even steeper than the climb he'd just made and he soon found the Nash's old brakes beginning to give way from overwork. There were horrible drop-offs beyond the metal rails edging the road and Burt had a few nasty moments when he feared the brakes would fail altogether.

He had read that many people were killed driving out of these mountains. The friction from the miles and miles of braking would cook a car's brakes before it got to the bottom and it would fail to slow down at the next corner it came to, plunging over the side. But years of driving the equally fearsome mountain passes of the South Island of New Zealand had taught Burt a trick or two. He held his door open as he drove, letting it act as an airbrake. It startled the cars coming the other way, but he found that even on the steepest sections, the Nash would not roll at more than 60 miles an hour with the door open. Before long he was safely bowling along on flat ground through a gentle forested landscape and by mid-afternoon he was standing on the Seattle docks.

The shipping agents assured him that the boxes containing the bike and trailer, being light, would have been loaded near the top of the cargo and could be easily unloaded. Smiling happily, he headed off to the customs department where he was told that, as the bike was a record-breaking machine, it must be worth a great deal of money. It would not be a problem issuing a permit for it to enter and leave the United States, but a bond of $10,000 cash would be required.

Burt was stunned. He walked outside, took a deep breath and then walked back in again. He explained his situation. He wasn't a big deal record breaker, he was just a bloke with an old motorcycle who had come to the United States to see how fast it could go, because there was nowhere back home long enough to get a decent run.

The customs agents searched through their rule books and in the end told Burt that what he needed was a lawyer. They handed Burt a list of names and let him use a phone in a spare office. The name McPherson leapt out at Burt for no better reason than it was Scottish, like his grandfather's. Burt rang the number.

McPherson turned out to work in a very big office at the very top of a very tall skyscraper. The view from the picture windows made Burt dizzy for a moment. Like all the officials Burt had already spoken to that day McPherson listened to Burt's story politely. Then, for two hours, he consulted a range of law books, occasionally asking Burt a question. Burt sat as silent as stone, desperately aware that he was paying for every minute he spent in the office. A lawyer who could afford a view like this was not going to be cheap. By the time McPherson gave a little grunt of satisfaction, Burt was in a cold sweat.

'Mr Munro. I believe I have found the solution to your problem. It would appear that your machine is essentially American in the eyes of the law, because it was manufactured here. There is no reason why it should not come home for as long as it likes with no bond whatsoever being required.'

He snapped the book shut and reached for his phone, instructing his secretary to get hold of the customs officials. He promised them a note explaining his opinion and suggested that they release the Indian at once.

Burt was in turmoil. The news was good . . . but how would he pay McPherson's fee? This was a disaster. He could see no point in delaying the awful moment so he thanked the lawyer and asked what he owed as calmly as he could. McPherson walked around the desk, guided Burt to the door with a friendly hand on his shoulder and told him he owed him nothing. He smiled for the first time since Burt had met him and offered his hand. 'It has been a pleasure,' he told Burt. 'I wish you the very best of Scottish luck.'

CHAPTER TWENTY-THREE

UTAH AT LAST

With the bike safely secured on the trailer Burt took off
again across the Cascade Mountains and on to Utah.
The next crisis occurred only 160 kilometres later when
the bolts holding the trailer's towbar fell out. Suddenly
the trailer and bike were swinging around on the safety
chain. The first inkling Burt had was when the Nash
began to sway all over the road. He managed to stop
without hitting anything and made temporary repairs,
which got him to the next gas station. The owner was so
taken with the visitor and his streamliner that he gave
Burt the nuts and bolts he needed for free.

He managed another 150-odd kilometres before the
car's hood suddenly flew open, completely blocking his
view of the road. Again he managed to stop safely and

The Munro Special on the trailer Burt built.

wired the hood shut before continuing. Unfortunately the engine needed a gallon of oil every 150 kilometres and now he had to untie the wire every time he wanted to open the hood. The metal rod that normally held the hood up had been destroyed when it flew open, so he used the oil dipstick to prop it up while he poured the oil. The third or fourth time he did this, he forgot the dipstick was there and tried to slam the hood down.

The dipstick bent like a bow and then fired itself, with perfect accuracy, right through the radiator. Burt suddenly found hot water gushing over his shoe. He removed the dipstick from the radiator and once more propped the bonnet open with it, berating it loudly. 'You could have hit the air cleaner, or the firewall, or the engine, or any bloody thing and instead you just had to hit something that would break!'

The road stretched out for ever in both directions in a sweltering, shimmering haze of heat. The only growing things in sight were stunted, spiny bushes and the odd half-dead tree. This part of the United States was famous for its potatoes. 'Crikey,' he muttered to himself, 'You couldn't grow a spud here, that's for sure.'

He began to cast about the roadside until he found a suitable stick. Sitting in the shade of the Nash he quickly whittled it into shape with his fruit-paring knife, creating a plug. He wrapped it in cloth and jammed it into the hole in the radiator. It slowed the leak down enough that Burt could drive ten kilometres before stopping to refill the radiator. Fortunately he always carried plenty of spare water.

In this way he limped to a small town called Mountain Home where he pulled up outside a diner. The car was steaming and Burt was, too, sweating like a man with a fever. Despite driving with all the windows down, the temperature in the car had been nearly unbearable and he was dizzy with the heat. A large thermometer fastened to the diner wall read 110 degrees Fahrenheit. A sign underneath it read 'It's cooler inside'.

Burt drained a long, cold Coke before chatting with the locals in his usual friendly fashion. They were as helpful as he had come to expect from Americans and directed him to a radiator repair man just out of town. The man fixed the leak while Burt told him all about his plans. When he had finished, the man warned him that the old radiator would no longer work as well as it had. 'Real hot days like today will be too much for it unless you take it easy.'

Burt thanked him and asked nervously how much it would cost. The man wanted only $4, which was the cost of the materials he had used. 'I enjoyed listening to you,' he told Burt, 'and I believe in paying for my entertainment. I hope you go real well at Bonneville.'

Burt was now behind schedule and in spite of his reluctance to drive at night he decided to press on. The night was impossibly hot and he still had to top up the radiator regularly. At some point he stopped to read a sign that informed him he had just passed into Utah. This heartened him somewhat, although about thirty kilometres from Wendover a passing car kicked up a rock, smashing one of his headlights and reducing visibility so much that he could only just make out the white line on the road. His already slow progress was reduced to little better than a crawl by the time he finally pulled into Wendover at three in the morning.

He booked a room at the State Line Motel and fell into bed, delighting in the crisp, clean sheets. He had arrived. Right now he was exhausted, but in the morning everything would be just fine.

CHAPTER TWENTY-FOUR

SPEED WEEK

Burt's first task on the salt was to pass the technical inspection. As he lined up with his bike many of those he had met over the years came to say hello and have a look. Burt demonstrated the snug fit of his shell and everyone agreed it looked crazy but quite cool. It was pretty sleek and it looked light. When Burt bent down so that the curve of his back blended with the curve of the shell there was a murmur of appreciation and he climbed out glowing with pride.

He was brought back to earth with a bump when somebody pointed out an area of white canvas on one of the tyres where he had sanded too enthusiastically. Having had some experience of this problem with inspectors at home, Burt was careful to make sure that when he finally rolled the bike in front of the officials, the offending patch ended up underneath. Passing the bike through inspection proved easier than passing himself.

Burt's old suit pants, shirt, worn-out sandshoes and battered leather jacket were the subject of a heated exchange. Burt insisted that he wore the gear because it was comfortable and if he was comfortable he would concentrate better, and that meant the gear made him safer. The argument went back and forth until the senior inspector finally said, 'Look, Mr Munro, none of this stuff offers any real protection if you crash. We just can't let you run like this.'

Burt fixed the man with a hard stare. 'I got married in these pants and they are high-quality, pure wool. Everybody knows wool is great for resisting flame. And I wear the sandshoes because otherwise I can't fit in. Besides, it's my flaming skin and bones, so what's your bloody problem?'

By now many of the friends Burt had made over his years of attending Speed Week had gathered around and there were murmurs of support. He pressed his advantage. 'Show me the rule that says I can't wear what I like!'

The inspector glared back. 'All right, you do what you want. But don't blame me when they carry you away in a box!'

Burt and his friend Rollie Free before Burt's first run.

Next Burt joined the queue of first-timers waiting to make a low-speed run in front of Speed Week's senior officials, who wanted to make sure the riders had control of their machines. The oldest of the officials was a chap called Earl Flanders.

Burt shook hands and introduced himself. Flanders nodded. 'Sorry about the wait, Mr Munro.' He took a long look at the little red streamliner. 'Now this looks real interesting. What you got under the hood?'

'I call her the Munro Special and she's half me and half 1920 Indian Scout.'

Flanders did not try to conceal his surprise. 'And how

fast are you hoping to go on this thing? If you want a record it would be, what, the 55-cubic-inch modified streamliner class? From memory that record's well over 170 miles an hour. You really think your old scooter can run anywhere near that?'

'I reckon we might,' Burt said slowly. 'We ran close to 150 on a road near home before we ran out of room.' He gazed out across the salt flats. 'That won't be a problem around here.'

Flanders nodded, suddenly satisfied. 'Okay, take her up to about 90 and we'll follow. We just want to make sure it's not gonna fall apart and you know what you're doing.' He turned to the others. 'Okay, guys, we're doing a safety run.'

And so Burt found himself riding on the salt where he discovered that at anything over 120 miles an hour his streamliner developed a sickening speed wobble that threatened to push him out of control. It was just as well he'd left the car full of officials behind when he opened her up in second gear. He had won the right to run, but the idea of running flat out with the thing weaving like a headless chicken was terrifying.

The drill for the week was that a number of bikes and cars would make their run one way, gathering at the far end for servicing before running back. The only other critical rule was that the return run had to be made within one hour of the first.

Burt was among the first to run and he was clearly nervous. He climbed awkwardly into the shell, lowering his body carefully so that his legs dropped into their aluminium cradles. Two of his friends were on hand to give him his push-start, but Burt pointed at two tall, well-built young men nearby and said he wanted them as his pushers instead. A little surprised at being dismissed in this manner, one of his friends asked Burt why. Because younger men run faster, said Burt.

The two lads were happy to oblige and when the time

Burt and his supporters on the salt.

came they pushed lustily, with Burt yelling at them to put more effort into it. But the bike refused to start and the new pushers were soon too exhausted to continue. Burt's friends stepped back in. Burt was so close to panic he was yelling at them to push faster before the wheels had even begun to roll.

They put their backs into it and this time the bike started immediately and sped away, leaving Burt's two friends sprawled face down in the salt. As they picked themselves up they saw him accelerate smoothly into the distance, his back level with the streamliner, head tucked down behind the tiny windscreen.

At ninety miles an hour Burt reached down and slipped the gear lever into second, rejoicing as the speed built up. At about 100 miles an hour the wobbling began again. As the bike accelerated up to about 140 he began to wonder if he might have to abort the mission. At 145 miles an hour he slipped the gear lever into third. The bike was seriously unbalanced now and it took every bit of skill Burt had, from nearly half a century of riding flat out, to keep it from tumbling right over. He kept the throttle wide open, desperately hoping the weave might go away at higher speed. It did not, but as he continued to accelerate it no longer seemed to be getting worse. Bugger it, he thought. It's all or nothing.

He was vividly aware that he was going extremely fast now. The interval between markers seemed to be nothing at all. As he approached the end of the timed sections his vision began to fade completely. Something was spattering onto his goggles, coating the lenses with a black, sticky substance. He could feel it stinging the exposed skin on his face, but the discomfort was insignificant compared with the terror of being unable to see the black line on the salt or the marker boards, or anything else for that matter. Thinking now only of survival and with no idea where he was or which direction he was travelling, he slowly wound the throttle off and let the bike coast, fighting the weave as the speed slowly bled away.

By now he had shot past the nine-mile marker where the previous competitors had gathered and drifted way out into the empty desert. Completely exhausted and disorientated, Burt remembered just in time to lower his landing gear as the bike finally spluttered to a halt, stalling in a patch of soft salt. He lifted his goggles and peered around, squinting against the glare for a clue to where he was. As far as he could see he was alone in the vastness, save for a shimmering black speck in the distance.

Way out on the salt a couple of young guys had been fooling around on a Norton, stopping from time to time to observe the speed attempts through a pair of binoculars. They had watched Burt streak past the finishing area and continue into the desert, and had correctly concluded that he was in trouble. They rode over and helped a grateful Burt pull the bike out of the shallow mush. Pointing him in the direction he needed to go, they pushed him off.

Burt's friends had waited for the other racers to go through before driving the Nash up to the assembly area to help Burt prepare for his return run. In case he had broken something they towed the trailer with them. At about the five-mile mark one of them noticed a wheel running along beside them. The wheel looked familiar. A quick glance behind them confirmed that the trailer was now missing one. To their horror the wheel began to curve off towards the course. 'God almighty,' one of them yelled. 'If that thing gets on the track we're in big trouble! What if it hits someone!'

The old Nash roared after the trailer wheel, which showed no signs of slowing. Eventually it began to run out of steam, executed a tight little turn and flopped over. Burt's friends let out a sigh of relief. A quick rifle through Burt's spare-parts box soon turned up a suitable nut they could use to fasten it back on the trailer.

By the time they got to the assembly point Burt had returned from his trip out into the desert and was busy cleaning the mysterious black substance that had blinded him from his goggles. He had obviously recovered his confidence. He now knew why his vision had failed. He had been blinded by fried rubber coming off his front tyre. Spinning at three times the speed it was designed for, it had expanded outwards until it rubbed against the bike. Tiny bits of rubber had flown backwards at high speed and coated his goggles. It was something he couldn't fix. He decided to press on regardless, hoping for better luck on the return run.

When his turn came the Indian started easily and his friends watched it accelerate smoothly away from

Burt and Team Indian.

their usual vantage point, sprawled on the salt in Burt's wake.

Out on the course Burt saw the seven-mile marker flick by and wondered how the devil he could have run that far already. Of course, he had only run two miles. He just did not realise that the numbers were now counting down, not up. As the speed built and built the terrible weave returned. To make matters even more hellish his vision was once more beginning to fade.

Burt Munro was fighting for his life and he was doing it as a true follower of the God of Speed: he was not even trying to slow down. He no longer had any idea where he was. He was simply determined to run until the bike broke or crashed. After what felt like many miles the engine faltered and dropped on to one cylinder, but still he kept going, not knowing if he was heading into the vast emptiness of the salt flats or aiming straight at a building. When the bike finally ran out of fuel Burt somehow remembered to deploy his landing gear and the bike slowly coasted to a halt, the diminishing sound of salt crunching under the tyres the only noise to break the perfect silence. Utterly exhausted he pushed his goggles up and once more looked about at a glaring, empty landscape. 'Don't tell me I'm lost again,' he croaked.

Wearily he unfolded himself from the shell and

examined his leg. For some time he had been vaguely aware that it was hurting; now it began to get really painful. The exhaust, which was shielded only by a thin metal and asbestos strip, had heated up so much during the long run that it had burnt him badly. His leg looked horrible.

In the meantime, Burt's two friends were making their way to the start line, stopping regularly to tighten the bolt on the trailer wheel, which kept trying to fall off. At the start area they could see no sign of Burt. Further enquiry revealed that Burt had in fact come through some time ago, the bike running flat out on one cylinder, and that he had disappeared in the general direction of Wendover.

The alarmed Munro Special Team gunned the Nash after Burt, stopping twice more to tighten the trailer wheel, until they finally came across the Indian, standing alone under the blazing sun. There was no sign of Burt, but when they crunched to a stop beside the stranded streamliner his head popped up from behind the bike where he had been sound asleep in the little patch of shade. 'Where have you buggers been hiding?' he demanded. 'I've been asleep here for hours. Gee, my leg hurts.'

They loaded the bike on to the trailer and headed back to the start-finish line, where a beaming Earl Flanders told

Burt that he had been timed at 178.971, a new national speed record.

Burt slumped back against the Nash and let the news sink in. He was a champion. He had had his run on the salt and he had set a record on his Indian.

'If that's the case,' he said grumpily, wincing at the pain in his leg, 'I'm never coming back here again.'

Even as he said it, he knew it wasn't true.

Back in Wendover a few years later Burt was full of confidence that he could not only set the record he wanted, but also shatter the 200 mile an hour barrier. But the God of Speed is a fickle fellow. During his qualifying run Burt was horrified to discover the streamliner was again shaking and weaving, even at his modest qualifying speed of 172 miles an hour. The next day he lined up to take his first serious run with frayed nerves and a sense of dread. But Burt always found confidence once he was under way. He took the bike up to about 180 miles an hour in spite of the shaking and weaving. It was an heroic effort, and far more than most mortals would have attempted. Still the God of Speed wanted more. As he approached the timed sections Burt had a split second to make his choice. Did he back off and hope he could slow the bike down without crashing, or did he go for it and hope it became more stable in the mysterious world that waited behind the door?

It was never really an issue. He kept the throttle wound hard against the stop. As he hit the timed miles the bike was going faster than it ever had before. At over 200 miles an hour, the first quarter mile went past in just four seconds.

The chief timekeeper, Otto Crocker, announced over the PA system that Burt had been travelling at well over 200 miles an hour through the timed quarter-mile section. Some said he'd put it at 212 miles an hour. Finally Burt could give up.

CHAPTER TWENTY-FIVE

THE PERFECT RUN

Some years later, a Highway Patrol officer was quietly minding his own business close to the Utah state border when a red projectile flashed past him at well over 100 miles an hour. He wheeled his car round and gave chase, finally coming across the red missile on the side of the road about four kilometres away. He took a good look at the rider, who seemed to be an elderly man, tinkering with something inside the strange red body.

'Do you have any idea how fast you were going, sir?' he asked.

'I sure do,' the old guy replied. 'It was a lousy 160 miles an hour at best.'

The officer was taken aback. 'Were you wanting to go faster?' He took a closer look at the machine. 'On that?'

The old fellow stood up and pulled a piece of cloth out of his pocket. He wiped his hands and mopped his face. 'I was hoping to, yes. But there's a problem I can't fix. I might as well go home to New Zealand and come back next year.' He sighed and shook his head. 'At least you can give me a ride back to my car. I'll drive back and put the Indian on the trailer.'

The officer was astonished. 'You mean that thing is an Indian motorcycle? And you want to go faster than 160 miles an hour on it?'

The strange old man laughed. 'I've already run at over 200 miles an hour. One hundred and sixty is like a stroll in the bloody park.'

The patrolman took another long look at the red streamliner, noting the narrow front tyre and the leaf-spring suspension. 'What year was this thing made?'

'I've made bits and pieces over the years,' the man replied, 'but the bike was built in 1920.'

'And what about you?'

'Born in 1899. Queen Victoria was on the throne and the sun was shining on the British Empire!'

The officer shook his head. 'I should be throwing you in jail, but I guess I'll just give you a ride back to your car.

No one would believe it if I told them what you just told me anyway.'

They were soon rolling back down the highway. The officer looked over at his passenger, who seemed somewhat downcast. 'Listen, old timer,' he said. 'I have a feeling you'll fix whatever it is and have that thing doing 200 miles an hour in no time. Just promise me you won't do it on my highway.'

Burt made ten trips to Speed Week in the end and kept on working on motorcycles and racing them well into his seventies. But the time came when his eyesight began to fail and he sold his tools and called it a day. He had grandchildren by now and he enjoyed spending time with them. The neighborhood kids continued to drop by whenever they liked for a biscuit and a yarn.

He had finally made the local council's life easier by moving out of his garage into a cosy little house. With the sun streaming in, he would sit in his old armchair, close his eyes and find himself back on the salt. The Indian would be humming along, everything operating in perfect harmony. The black line would be flickering under the bike as it hurtled along, rock steady at maximum revs in top, doing well over 200 miles an hour. He would raise his head just a bit against the pressure of the slipstream and lift his eyes to take in the pure blue sky. As he drifted into sleep his perfect run would slowly fade, until there was nothing but the glittering white plain and the distant purple hills and perfect, eternal silence.

Legend of Speed: Burt at home in Invercargill with his first love.